T.L. OSBORN

The MESSAGE *that* WORKS

WHAT WE HAVE TOLD MILLIONS IN 73 NATIONS FOR 53 YEARS

Publisher

OSFO International
World HQ: Box 10, Tulsa, OK 74102 USA
Tel: (918) 743-6231
Fax: (918) 749-0339
E-Mail: OSFO@aol.com

Canada: Box 281, Adelaide St. Post Sta., Toronto M5C 2J4
England: Box 148, Birmingham B3 2LG
(A Registered Charity)

I DEDICATE THIS book to those —

*WHO are weary of condemnation,
insecurity, confusion and guilt;*

WHO feel alone and without personal value;

*WHO want a new lifestyle of happiness, health,
purpose and blessing;*

*WHO face problems, pressures and dilemmas,
and who crave practical answers;*

*WHO desire forgiveness for wrongs committed
against God, against others,
and against themselves;*

*WHO have been frustrated by doctrines
of evil spirits in Christians and need
to know they are secure in Christ;*

*WHO need healing for the whole person,
mental, physical, and spiritual.*

✧ ✧ ✧

*THIS BOOK publicizes a rich legacy of
Seven gifts,
Seven blessings,
Seven treasures,
Seven revelations*
for real LIVING

The Foundation of our MESSAGE to the World

T.L. OSBORN

*B*IBLE QUOTATIONS in this book are derived
from the King James Version unless otherwise
noted. (References are included.) They are sometimes personalized, paraphrased or abridged to facilitate clarity and to encourage individual application. We have taken the liberty of conforming them,
in structure, to the person and tense of their contextual application.

The Author

ISBN 0-87943-095-8
Copyright 1997 by T.L. Osborn
Printed in the United States of America
All Rights Reserved

CONTENTS

SECTION VII
VICTORY RETRIEVED

What The Fight Of Faith IS
(Issue No.I)

What The Fight Of Faith Is AGAINST
(Issue No.II)

What IS The ARMOR Of God
(Issue No.III)

Come Back From The Dead

(Introduction)

For MORE THAN a half century, my wife, Dr. Daisy, and I have spoken to millions of people, face to face, in nearly eighty nations of the world. This book contains the foundation for the seven preeminent truths we have shared during fifty-three years of ministry together.

I have titled this book, *The MESSAGE That WORKS* because what we have taught has created a better world. Millions have been lifted out of despair, disease, hopelessness and confusion. We publish these biblical expositions so that their miracle working influence can bless your life too.

Seed Concepts That *Work* Wonders

There is no magic about these concepts. They work because they are strategic, dynamic, pragmatic — and biblical. They will work in your life from the time that you comprehend them, as good seeds grow from the time they are planted.

The essential Gospel has been complicated by religion. But its truths are simple. With knowledge of a few fundamentals one can be blessed supernaturally, abundantly. This book contains seven truths to meet the seven needs of your life. They will procreate their wonders in you while you read them. They embody *glad tidings of good things* Ro.10:15 to bless you as they have enriched millions of others.

I have written this book for ordinary people who are tired of religious ambiguity and who want a relationship with God based on confidence and love, not on condemnation and fear.

Contextual Application
Of Bible References

The hundreds of Bible quotations that are included (with references indicated) are sometimes paraphrased or abridged to facilitate clarity. You will notice that we have taken the liberty of conforming them, in structure, to the *person* and *tense* of their contextual application.

As you become aware of these seven concepts, you will experience a new beginning with God. If religious confusion and spiritual despair have dimmed your courage, destroyed your hope and left you numb, you can receive the greatest miracle of all. You can come back from the dead!

In our worldwide ministry, Daisy and I have observed the dehumanizing influence of despair. We have been messengers of hope to millions. They have lived again. What we have shared is so simple that professionals often miss it, yet it has given new life to multitudes around the world. It could be that destiny is at work in your choice to read this book.

Facts That Are *Global*

When we preach or write, we often relate miracles and experiences that we have witnessed. There are none in this book. It contains only *The MESSAGE That WORKS.*

To come back from the dead, one needs more than stories. One needs facts—the kind that are global, that work in any village, family or society, that are international, that are not americanized— that reveal God in the present, at your side, full of love, eager to bless and lift you so that you can share His Life with Him.

You may be a Moslem, Hindu, Animist, Buddhist, Shintoist, Catholic, Jew, Protestant, or you may claim no religion; You may live in a village or a refugee camp, a city or a town, a hut or an apartment, a straw shelter or a mansion; You may be male or female, rich or poor, lord or peasant,

citizen or president. Whatever your social, economic, national or religious status, these seven
cardinal concepts will engender in you a new
beginning with a new kind of Life.

Our Awakening Began In India

Most of the people we have addressed have
been in *non*-Christian nations. Our worldwide
odyssey began in India as young missionaries
where we were unprepared to cope with ancient
religions and before we understood Christ's
miracle power. We could not convince the people
of historic India about the Christian Gospel.

We returned home, profoundly disheartened,
feeling we had failed. Within a few months, we
experienced four visions that changed the course
of our lives.

Events That Changed Our Lives

The first vision: We heard a great conference
speaker at the Assemblies of God Campmeeting
in Brooks, Oregon, the Rev. Hattie Hammond.
She was ministering in the place of Dr. Charles S.
Price following his demise. Her subject was: *If
You Ever See Jesus, You Can Never Be The Same
Again.*(Inspired by The Gospel of John, Chapter One)

We drove home wiping tears to see the road.
The next morning at six o'clock, the first vision

took place. Jesus walked into our bedroom, not on the floor, but in the air. I saw Him in the same way that I see any person. I lay there unable to move a finger or a toe. Water poured from my eyes, yet I was not conscious of weeping.

After a long while, I was able to move myself onto the floor where I remained, face down before the Lord in prayer until the afternoon. When I was able to stand again and come out of that room, I was a changed person.

In India Daisy and I had witnessed the emptiness of religion without Life. But now, as I embraced her, I said, "Darling, we are not representing an empty religion, but a living, resurrected Christ." *I saw JESUS in that first vision.*

The second vision: Gordon Lindsay had organized an area wide Gospel campaign in Portland, Oregon. William Branham preached and prayed for the sick. Hundreds of people accepted Christ and we witnessed, for the first time, amazing and instantaneous healing miracles. *In that second vision, we saw Jesus at work IN A PERSON.*

The third vision: Following that meeting, we returned to our house and talked for hours. We wept together and pledged, "We shall read the Gospels as though we never heard of them before. Whatever Jesus says He will do, we will expect Him to do it. Whatever He says we can do, we will act on His Word and do it." *So our third vision was discovering Jesus IN HIS WORD*.

The fourth vision: Following that experience, we made announcements inviting the public to bring sick people to Montavilla Tabernacle, the church we pastored at the corner of Southeast 80th and Washington Streets in Portland. The old tabernacle was packed. We preached, then prayed for the sick, and it seemed that everyone we touched was instantly healed.

That was our fourth vision: We discovered Jesus at work IN US.

Our New Beginning

We sold our possessions and set out on our world saga, informing multitudes of the power and love of Jesus Christ. Over a half century has now come and gone.

My beloved wife, Daisy, transcended her mortal life on May 27, 1995. I will soon complete a book written in her memory entitled *DAISY — Her Triumph, My Trauma, Our Treasure*. Almost every married couple will be separated someday. In this book I have shared the lessons that I have learned — lessons that have sustained me through this dark valley of loneliness — lessons that have stabilized me as I have desperately tried to discover who this man, T.L. Osborn, is—*without Daisy.*

It has been calculated that Dr. Daisy and I may have preached to more people in *non-*Christian nations and have possibly witnessed more healing miracles than any other couple in history—not because of special faith, but because we have proclaimed the Gospel together to so many multitudes in so many nations for so many years.

Java Or Colombia – The Same

A elderly gentleman visited our recent crusade in Colombia, South America. He had helped us in 1954 when our public Gospel crusades in Djakarta and Surabaya, Java ignited the first great spiritual awakening in Indonesia. He said that the Colombia Crusade was the same as he remembered the Java Crusades to be—the same anointing, the same message, the same miracle confirmation.

That is because *Jesus Christ is the same, yesterday, today and forever.*[Heb.13:8] The Gospel is unchanged. The same apostolic ministry witnessed in Bible days is God's will for today. He says, *I am the Lord, I change not.*[Mal.3:6]

Life-Long Success Secret

In our teaching seminars and campaigns of evangelism, leaders often ask, "What is the secret to the long success of your ministry to so many multitudes in so many nations?"

We have always responded: "We teach Good News. Our message is simple but fundamental. We acquaint people with: 1) Their origin in God, 2) Satan's deception, 3) Christ's death and resurrection and what that means, and 4) The reality of His Life today in believers."

No *non*-Christian religion offers forgiveness for sins, healing for diseases, security for fear, hope for despair, solutions for problems, relief for pain, *Life* for death — *transformation*. These blessings comprise the essence of Christ's Gospel. That is why people of all religions are attracted to our campaigns. They listen, they believe, they receive and they are blessed.

Millions live in a quandary about God. They seek peace and consolation through religion, philosophy, incantations, self-sacrifice, penance, superstition, and other avenues of spiritual quest.

Thousands of times we have witnessed that when people comprehend the seven truths expressed in this book, new hope and happiness, life and love, peace and power are birthed in them. They come back from the dead with a new beginning for real living. That can take place in you as you journey through his book.

The Message—The Power

The message of the Gospel in its *simplicity* [2Co.11:3] is the only answer to the dilemmas and delusions of hurting people.

Human beings experience seven basic needs. God reveals Himself in seven ways to meet those needs. Each provision He offers is made available by the death of Christ. They are available to every person of every race and color in every nation.

In the seven distinct sections of this book, beginning at chapter fifteen, we have set forth humanity's seven fundamental needs and God's seven redemptive provisions.

Each section delineates one of the seven human deficiencies resulting from Adam and Eve's sin. Each section expounds the redemptive work of Christ that provides for each inadequacy. He has ransomed humankind from their fallen state and has reconciled people to God as His friends and partners. Therefore, each human need has been re-provided by God's grace in redemption.

Each of the seven sections begins in the Garden of Eden because each human dilemma has its roots in Adam and Eve's sin. Then each section ends in our reconciliation to Christ through His vicarious work of redemption on our behalf.

Four Facts That Comprise The *Gospel*

For more than a half century, Daisy and I have dedicated the finest years of our lives to telling people the four facts that comprise the Gospel: 1) God's creation, 2) Satan's deception, 3) Christ's substitution, and 4) Our restoration or salvation. Paul said, *The Gospel IS the power of God unto salvation to everyone that believes.*[Rom.1:16]

Announcing these Gospel facts projects or transmits God's power into people. When these truths are heard, faith is born.[Rom.10:17] When they are embraced, God's Holy Spirit *confirms* them [Mar.16:20] and miracles result. That will take place in your life as you read this book. Whether you hear truth or read truth, its power is the same. Jesus said, *You shall know the truth and the truth shall make you free.*[Joh.8:32]

The *Seed* – Better Than The *Touch*

In our ministry to multitudes, we never touch people when we pray for their healing. Although it is scriptural,[Mar.16:18; Luk.4:40] trying to lay hands on suffering people in a multitude can provoke panic and result in injury to them.

We publicly announce the facts of the Gospel. The people listen and believe. The good seeds are planted in their lives. When they embrace Christ as Savior, they are transformed, and in tens of thousands of cases, their sicknesses and maladies are miraculously cured too. The seed produces its harvest. That can take place in your life as you grasp the truths presented here.

This book contains the essence of what we have told, and of what I continue telling, multitudes and individuals alike. It is *The MESSAGE That WORKS.*

CHAPTER ONE

GOD'S GOOD PLAN

GOD CREATED ADAM AND EVE and placed them in a garden of abundance where everything that He made was *pleasant and good.*[Gen.1:31; 2:9] They were His companions and they experienced His fullness.

In God's redemptive plan for human lives, He still wants every person to have happiness and pleasure, energy and strength, peace and love, tranquillity and joy, health and dignity, and an abundance of real living.

But a tragedy interrupted rapport between God and people. The result is that now this world is filled with people fighting depression, struggling to meet obligations, plagued by disease and loneliness, abandoned and insecure—frustrated by problems without solutions.

23

Many have made irreparable mistakes and have engendered enemies. The psychological diseases of resentment, animosity, pride, jealousy, dishonesty and hatred have obstructed success and destroyed happiness in millions of lives.

Start A Miracle Today

God has made provision for every need or desire that you can experience. Start believing that He cares as much for you as He does for anyone else. Despite your shortcomings, God is on your side. A small grain of faith will start a miracle in your life today.

The Garden of Eden exhibited the lifestyle and circumstances for which God designed you.

On these pages, you will discover the road that leads back to the paradise that was forfeited so long ago by our foreparents, Adam and Eve.

Jesus Christ came to show us what God wants us to have. He opened to us the door of His limitless mercy and abundance, through His death on the Cross. Every miracle He performed was an example of what God wills for every other person in similar circumstances.

Miracle Examples For Us

When Jesus encountered people who were troubled by evil they had committed against themselves, their neighbors and God, He performed a *spiritual* miracle in their lives. He forgave them.^{Mar.2:5-7; Luk.7:47-48; 19:8-10; Joh.8:3-11}

When He came in contact with people who were suffering diseases or who were crippled or paralyzed, He performed *physical* miracles. He healed their bodies.^{Mat.8:16-17; 9:35 Mar.6:55-56; Luk.4:40}

When He found people who faced material needs, He performed *material* miracles. He provided for them — even when it required a creative miracle. ^{Mat.14:15-21; 17:24-27}

The Deadly Destroyer

Jesus said, *Satan's purpose is to steal, to kill and to destroy. My purpose is to give life in all its fullness.*
^{Joh.10:10 LB}

STEALING is taking something that belongs to someone else. Satan has done that by conditioning people's minds to accept poverty, fear, sickness, defeat and problems. Through this negative process they have been cheated out of God's bountiful provisions.

KILLING is cutting short someone's life. The devil has done that to millions through disease and fear, want and distress, tension and failure.

DESTROYING means to spoil and render useless something of value. The plagues of loneliness and poverty, of sickness and evil, of fear and of insecurity have destroyed the influence and happiness of millions whom God intended to be blessed with His fullness.

Ministry Of The Master

Jesus came to reveal God to us,[Joh.5:30; 6:38; 14:8-9] and to show us the kind of life He wills for us. He came to solve our problems, to forgive our sins, to heal our diseases, to give us success, to walk with us, to surround us with good things, to give us energy and to fill us with love and real Life.

Spiritually, God wills that we have peace, tranquillity, faith, hope, love, creativity and abundant living.

Physically, He wills healing, energy, physical strength and vigorous health.

Materially, He wills success, achievement, prosperity and access to the Divine Source of all material provisions.

Through His death on our behalf, Christ opened the way for us to come back to God, and for Him to come home to us.[Joh.14:23; 2Co.6:18]

CHAPTER TWO

CONNECTED WITH GOD

TRADITIONAL RELIGION has fostered a limited concept of God's relationship with people. It suggests that intimacy with Him is reserved for only those who live in self-imposed poverty and self-abasement.

You will discover seed-truths in this book that will extricate you from the religious syndrome of mediocrity that has proliferated through the centuries.

Discover The *New-Life* Force

On these pages, you will grasp God's purpose for you. You will gain understanding of your infinite value. You will discover your innate potential for happiness, health, success, and wholeness.

Alive in you, Jesus Christ becomes a new life-force that will not only produce blessings for yourself, but also for others.

This takes place in you as you learn these seven fundamental truths. Your thoughts and your words have the mysterious power of creating the situation that surrounds you. They are the seeds that you sow and they procreate of their kind.

This book will help you realize God's opinion of you. You will discover your roots in Divine Royalty. You will learn to think of yourself as God thinks of you, and to talk of yourself as He does — in the Bible.

God's miraculous power will be ignited within you. As His seeds of truth and faith are planted in you, they will produce His kind of person.

His Rainbow Of Fullness

Now that you have begun this book, be conscious of God's love and of the ransom He has paid for you. Be sensitive to how much it has cost Him to make His abundance available to you. Respond with veneration and with a hearty "Yes!" to each truth as you grasp it.

When you perceive God's abundance and begin to comprehend that He created the wealth of this world for the blessing of His children, the prison walls of the mind will crumble and the rainbow of His fullness will appear.

We must update our thinking and break the chains of centuries-old theology that links poverty to godliness, burdens to humility, and suffering to sainthood. We can pursue life with a fresh, God-inspired attitude. We can move ahead with the new, miracle energy that flows inside of us as we gain vital knowledge about God's will for us.

It's Not Too Good To be True

When Moses was ready to possess the rich land God had prepared for His people, he sent twelve spies to investigate.(Numbers, Chapter 13-14)

The majority of them took one look at that wealthy land and fled. They said in essence, "That land is too good to be true! It flows with milk and honey! It cannot be for us! Besides, giants are there! We saw them! We felt like grasshoppers! They could destroy us!"

They thought that way. They talked that way. They acted that way. Consequently, they reaped that crop. They never inherited the blessings God intended for them to share. They died in despair.

Only two men perceived things with God's perspective. Caleb and Joshua saw a land of blessing. Their assessment was: "This is a good land full of abundance. Since we are God's people, we can take it. He wants us to be enriched by it." God's promises were the source of their faith and of their courage. They acted according to their faith, and they inherited the rich Land of Promise.

Caleb and Joshua believed that rich land belonged to royalty. They were not content to leave it under the control of wasters. They were connected with God by their faith—and He prospered their way.

That will happen to you while you are reading this book. These seven divine seeds of blessing are going to be planted in the soil of your believing heart, and they will produce their rich harvest in your life.

Chapter Three

God's Kind
Of Being

In THE LAND of the Gadarenes, lived a demon-possessed man. The Bible says: *No one could bind him, not even with chains which he plucked asunder and broke.*[Mar.5:3-5] Demons gave him super physical strength.

David said, *The Lord is the strength of my life.*[Psa. 27:1] If devils could make a man physically strong enough to break chains and fetters, the Lord can impart physical strength to His children.

When you receive Jesus Christ, you are endowed with new energy. Learn the power of His presence. You cannot lose when God is your friend.

Disease, pain, failure and suffering are from a different source than what is beginning to flow inside you now. You are being joined with Deity.

The *gates of hell cannot prevail against you* ^{Mat.16:18} because God is on your side. Let your miracle begin right now. Open the doors of your mind to God's way of thinking. Disease and pain are not part of His plan. Poverty and lack do not bring glory to Him. He is the Source of abundance. He is the Creator. He owns everything. And you are His kind of being.

Breaking The Destructive Grip

In the past, you may have been conditioned to conformity and indigence, to sickness and failure, to depression and despair, to loneliness and dejection. Break the grip of these destructive influences and move ahead with God by identifying with His redemptive blessings.

Your small faith is enough to displace the mountains around you.

Your enemy never wanted you to discover the truths that are contained in this book because they will lead you to God's abundance and indomitable energy. It is no accident that this information has come into your hands.

The discoveries you make through reading this book will produce a wealth of blessing in your life and in the lives of those around you. Your thoughts and words will become good seeds and they will procreate God's good things.

Today a new power is starting to flow in you. You will begin to realize that God's plan for you is practical and powerful, and that it is the way to real Life.

Chapter Four

Beginning Inside

EACH SECTION OF this book ends with a Prayer Confession. As you read them aloud, they will familiarize your tongue and imprint your spirit with these powerful concepts. As a result, you will automatically adopt new thought patterns and new human behavior.

You will strike a gold mine of values that will enhance your quality of life. Happiness, success, health and blessing will begin to materialize around you. The Bible says: *Blessings shall come upon you and overtake you.*[Deu.28:2RSV] If you travel forty miles per hour, these blessings will travel fifty miles per hour to overtake you.

Words, Thoughts and Deeds
Are The *Seeds* Of Your Life

The situation that slowly but surely evolves around you is the harvest of the seeds that you have planted. What you think, say and do are the seeds that you constantly sow.

Wise and successful people understand that to change their environment, the change must begin inside themselves.

God has provided for you every blessing that you can need or desire—in seed form. All you have to do is plant the seeds—first in yourself, (that will happen as you read this book), then in others' lives around you by what you think, say and do.

Thoughts precede both words and actions, so change begins as one's thinking is reformed. Paul urged: *Be transformed by the renewing of your mind,*[Rom.12:2] *being conformed to the image of Christ*[Ro.8:29] *by the light of the knowledge of God in Jesus Christ.*[2Co.4:6] This book provides vital knowledge.

When new thoughts are formed within our minds through learning truth, they work their way and wield their influence outwardly from us. Change in us and around us results from the knowledge we plant within ourselves, not from the influence or circumstances outside of us.

We can only change ourselves. (We cannot change others.) Improvement takes place in ourselves as we take into ourselves the right information. Automatically we become what has been planted within us. The seed engenders and produces of its own kind. It procreates itself.

Chapter Five

The Mysterious Power

THE WISEST MAN who ever lived said, *My child,* **attend** *(apply your* **mind***) to my words; incline your* **ear** *to my sayings. Let them not depart from your* **eyes***; keep them in the midst of your* **heart***.*^{Pro. 4:20-21}

The blessings of happiness, success, health and peace are given to us by God in seed-form. He has invested His seed-truths with the miraculous power to procreate themselves—always in multiplied form.

By comprehending the simple truths presented in this book, you can experience the abundant blessings God has placed on this planet. It has never been His will that His children should live in spiritual, physical or material poverty.

You can realize health instead of living in malady and disease.

You can know peace instead of living under the pressure of guilt, fear and condemnation.

You can prosper instead of living in penury.

You can be a winner instead of a loser.

Seed Truths That Work Like Miracles

We were in our early twenties when Daisy and I became aware of the principles of God's *redemptive* blessings. During the last half-century, we have shared these truths with millions and they have created a better world. Now I publish them in this book so that thousands who have never heard us teach can be enriched and blessed.

Allow these divine seeds to be planted in your own life as you read and positively respond to the truths expounded in this book. They will work in you like miracles from God.

They will grow in any neighborhood. Economic crises cannot affect them.

They will produce their harvest under any form of government.

Plagues, holocausts, famines or depressions cannot stop their growth.

Transforming Power

The truths in this book will transform arrogance into loveliness and failure into success. Sickness will give way to a new source of invigorating health. Destructive and negative thoughts will yield to the positivism of a believer with faith in God.

CHAPTER SIX

GOD AT WORK

GOD IS GOOD. He wants everyone to enjoy His goodness and His abundant blessings.

We have shared the miracle-love of God with multitudes of from twenty thousand to three hundred thousand people and more, nightly, during more than a half century.

We have proven, thousands of times, that God is what He says He is, that He will do what He says He will do, that the Bible is real and that what it says is true. It works.

The Christian religion has become formalized by theological traditions derived from medieval concepts. As a result, much of society relegates God and miracles to legend or to superstition.

Instead of relating Him to the practical needs of humanity, religious people tend to limit Him to the ambiance of their church sanctuaries. (By "religious," I mean people who only know the rituals of Christianity without the reality of Christ's living presence in people today.)

Every time I see cancers healed, cripples walk, blind and deaf people restored; every time I see unhappy lives changed, unbelievers transformed, or poverty-stricken families discover God's abundance, I see *Him* at work. I see the miracle of His divine seeds procreating themselves.

India Changed Our Perspective

My wife and I went to India as young missionaries. We wanted to share the blessings of Jesus Christ with those who had not heard His Gospel. We had not yet learned the secrets of child-like faith and there were no miracles to confirm our teaching of the Good News.

But our own lives were positively affected even though we left India deeply discouraged. We had seen the masses of people benumbed by religion, without hope and without Life. We yearned for God's solution.

Then the Lord Jesus Christ appeared to me in a vision and in the aftermath of that awesome experience, the Bible became a living book to us. We discovered the principles of God's redemptive plan and how His miracle power is contained in the Gospel seeds that He has given us to plant.

Jamaica Experience

Our lives were re-focused. In the wake of that experience our first mission abroad took us to the Island-nation of Jamaica in the Caribbean.

For thirteen weeks, we ministered there. We counted a hundred and twenty-five deaf-mutes who were healed, over ninety totally blind people who received their sight, hundreds of lame and crippled people who were restored, and most significant of all, nearly ten thousand people who came forward and accepted Jesus Christ as their Savior.

Since that venture, we have communicated Christ's Gospel to millions of people in *non-*Christian nations, as Paul did, experiencing the same miraculous results that are recorded in the *Acts of the Apostles.*

As I recall the signs, wonders and miracles that we have witnessed in so many nations, I become so happy that I want to tell everybody in the whole world about God's Good News. The Psalmist urged, *Make known his deeds among the people.*[Ps.105:1]

That is the reason for publishing this book. It is our way of sharing with you the same blessings that you would receive if you were in the midst of one of our mass evangelism crusades abroad.

CHAPTER SEVEN

WHEN THE LIGHT TURNS ON

I WISH THAT all the world could know how good God is. The Bible says, *The Lord is gracious and full of compassion.*[Psa.86:15; 111:4; 112:4; 145:8] Jesus was everywhere *moved with compassion.*[Mat.9:36; 14:14; 18:27; Mar.1:41; 6:34] Another Bible verse says, *His compassions fail not.*[Lam.3:22]

Thirty-three times in the Bible book of Psalms it is stated, *His mercy endureth forever.*

For You, Lord, are good, and ready to forgive; and plenteous in mercy unto all them that call upon You.[Psa.86:5]

God says, *I will rejoice over you to do you good... with my whole heart and with my whole soul.*[Jer.32:41]

God has a very big heart and soul, and it all rejoices over *you* to do you good.

God Is Not A Tyrant

Many people think of God as a dominating master who lords it over people with a whip, afflicting and punishing them with sickness, suffering, poverty and failure. This is not true. God wills that people enjoy His lifestyle of happiness, success and blessing—physically, emotionally, spiritually and materially.

After you have read this book, you will tend to forget the negative way you formerly thought. The biblical concepts in this book will obliterate from your mind out-moded and negative thought-patterns. You will be *transformed by the renewing of your mind.*[Rom.12:2] *Your understanding will be enlightened and you will know the riches of His inheritance in His followers and the greatness of His power to us who believe — the power that was wrought in Christ when God raised Him from the dead.*[Ep.1:18-20]

God created Adam and Eve *in His own image,*[Ge.1:26-27; 5:1-2] to be like Himself. That is why people search for some form of spiritual connection with what they may call *The Creator, The Divine* or *Omnipotent* or *Universal* or *Cosmic One.* They search through mysticism, philosophy, empty religion, self-negation, penitence, or other ceremonial rituals, both secretly and publicly.

This book shows *The Way* to friendship, fellowship, and partnership with God.

The Worldwide Search

Around the world, whether on the busy streets of Paris, New York or Bogota, or in the villages and cities of the Philippines, India, China and Africa, humanity searches for a living deity. It is written on their faces and expressed in the way they walk. They would give anything to know that God is real or to see evidence that He cares about them.

A Hindu business man said, "I would like to believe that there is a god of some kind, somewhere, but I have no reason to think that one would help me or would even know about me."

An Eastern philosopher said, "There is no way for human persons to know The Universal One. *It* is unmanifest, unthinkable, and unapproachable — absolute *im*personality."

A Hindu teacher said, "If there were a God, He would be too impersonal to be of any use to me, and I really think it would be the greatest of sins to disturb Him on my behalf."

These statements express the heart cry of millions. We have journeyed abroad and have looked into the faces of confused and despairing multitudes around the world. Our mission has been to share with them the simple but powerful truths of God's Love. We call it the Good News, the Gospel.

I have watched the light turn on in tens of thousands of faces as they have been made aware that God cares for them.

Psychological Infirmities That Destroy Human Persons

God is not a destroying Deity who sends infirmity and pain. Luk.9:56; Psa.34:8; 145:8-10; Nah.1:7; Rom.2:4 He does not will poverty and lack in people's lives. His fullness is for all who follow Him. Jer.2:7; Joe.2:26; Ecc.5:18-19; Mat.25:29; 1Sam.2:7-8; Pro.8:17-18;10:22; 28:19-20; Psa.34:10; 68:19; 104:24,28; 112:1,3; 3Jn.2; 1Chr.29:11-12

People plagued by guilt and inner fears poison their own systems and often seed themselves for disease and deterioration. They permit their lives to be devastated by the psychological traumas of hatred, jealousy, envy and greed, which are forms of self-abuse and of self-destruction.

Their lack of faith in God, in their neighbors, and in themselves causes them to attract defeat, confusion and decadence.

Capable and talented people permit their lives to be wasted. The plague of poverty curses millions who live in a world of abundance.

Bodies that should be vibrant and healthy in service to God and others, deteriorate by inactivity, disease and depression.

The gnawing, noxious cancers of negativism, resentment, remorse and despair poison the life streams of thousands who could otherwise be channels of love and blessing to humanity.

God is good and He wills only good for people. He is Life and He yearns for them to share the Life He has made available. He created human persons *in His own image* Gen.1:26-27; 5:1-2 so that makes you and me His kind of being.

CHAPTER EIGHT

MAKING NEW DISCOVERIES

NOTHING IS MORE vital to a person's self-esteem than to discover one's own value.[Luk.12:6-7; Psa.8:4-6] Every human is a creation of *God who is Love.*[1Jo.4:8,16] People are the product of Love. This is why hatred and fear are so destructive in human lives. *There is no fear in Love; but perfect Love casts out fear.*[1Jo.4:18]

Every human person has divine purpose. God paid a great price for each individual. He wants people near Him. He believes in people just as they are.[Mat.6:26; 12:12; Joh.3:16; 1Co.6:20; 1Pe.1:18-19; Rev.1:5] He has opened the way for you and me to be successful, happy, productive and abundantly blessed.

Some imagine that the process will be painful. In one sense it may be, because of one's need to adjust thinking, to adopt new ideals and perhaps to reform language and action patterns. Those things can be painful if change seems threatening, offensive or unsettling.

Rigidity or Flexibility

People often develop lifestyles and attitudes which develop harmful habits and thought patterns. They decide who and what are to blame for their problems, almost always excusing themselves. It is difficult for them to realize that their own thoughts, words and deeds are the seeds of their own successes or failures, of their own environment, pleasant or painful, and even of their own physical conditions.^{Pro.6:2; 21:23; Psa.141:3; Jam.1:26;} ^{1Pe.3:10; Col.4:6; Pro.15:23; Phi.4:7; 2Ti.1:7; 2Co.10:5; Phi.4:8; Isa.26:3}

By adjusting one's thinking, vocabulary and actions, anyone can recreate their own environment.

Adapting to *His* Way

With a fresh look at life from God's viewpoint, you can discover the wonderful life that He wills for you. Then as you adapt to His Way, you can experience real Life as God planned it for you. This book will show you *The Way.*

The greatest insurance on earth is to be connected with God. You cannot fail with Him as your partner.[Isa.41:10; 54:17; 55:10-11] His covenant guarantees His blessings.[Deu.28:1-4; Psa.89:34; 1Ki.8:56]

The stock market may crash. Wars may rage. Tragedies may occur. Famines, droughts, or material crises may ravage society. But when you are in tune with God, you will not be defeated because He wills His best for His children.

Assimilating Truth

As you read these chapters, the truths they convey will become part of you. They will affect your attitude and your perspective in life.

Resolve to embrace these concepts: 1) God is good and rich and loving; 2) He does not punish with disease, pain and failure; 3) He never desires poverty or lack or need; 4) He longs to share His love and health and abundant life with people; 5) He believes in *you* — just as you are.

Re-Focused Outlook

By the time you have finished the seven faith-building sections of this book, your perspective will be re-focused. The blessings of God's abundant living will become evident in and around you because of the good seeds you will have planted in yourself. They will produce their good harvest in your life, and in the lives of others around you.

The Good News (or Gospel) is *good tidings of good things, the publishing of salvation that God reigns.*[Rom.10:15; Isa.52:7]

That is what our world ministry is all about, and it is the reason for this book that publicizes *The MESSAGE That WORKS.*

Chapter Nine

Without Clichés
Or Bigotry

A FRENCH TEACHER, spending her vacation in America, visited our International Headquarters in Tulsa, Oklahoma.

Since she spoke practically no English, the receptionist called our French translator to host the lady on her tour of our premises.

Impacted by her visit to this world ministry, she began to pose questions about our *"programme d'evangelisation, religion et doctrine."*

Our translator took advantage of the questions to witness about Christ. She explained the simplicity of our faith: It is Jesus, not a religion, but a Person, the Son of God, who died for our sins, who was raised for our justification, and who gives us Eternal Life. She emphasized that we can have daily fellowship with God in our lives now.

Questions From France

To the French lady, this seemed too simple to be valid. Her questions were typical of today's world: "Why evangelize people of other lands such as Hindus, Buddhists, Moslems? They are content in their own religions. How do we know that ours is any better?

"How can we know that God exists, that Jesus is His Son, or that He was born of a virgin? Why was His death any different from that of any other good man, or His blood any more divine than that of any other prophet or sadhu or holy man? How can we be sure that He was raised from the dead?

"Doesn't it seem that life is without purpose and leads to final nothingness? How can one be sure that there is any truth to the Bible?"

She Assured Us That
She Was Not A Pagan

Then, of course, to reassure her hostess that she was not a pagan, she explained, "You know, I have my religion. I feel it's important for children to receive their 'First Communion.' After all, we aren't savages! But anyone who thinks or reads or has average intelligence, must ask questions. You see, I'm a divorcee with two children to raise. I wonder about raising them without a father to face an unfortunate future. Why not just end it, once and for all?

"But if there is a God, and if He is good, why does He permit so much misery and sickness? Why are innocent children born with defects, crippled, etc.? If God can do miracles, why does He not cure everyone? Probably there is a devil. That would explain a lot of things! But 'original sin by Adam and Eve'? Isn't that the issue of sexual relations between men and women?

"The Bible talks of a tree whose fruit was forbidden, of how Adam and Eve deliberately chose to disobey God and of how they ate the forbidden fruit. Consequently, sin, evil and suffering are the results. I suppose that's logical.

Hope In Jesus, *The Way*

"But, if I simply follow your counsel and ask Jesus to come into my heart and guide me and live in me day after day, what are the prayers I should recite? What are the sins I should abstain from? To just come to Jesus, as I am, and ask Him to come and live in me? Is that all? It seems too simple. I think one should first improve oneself. As a divorcee, am I automatically condemned by the church? Can I be helped?

"In my predicament, are you saying I can pray and know God and talk to Him as a friend? As a father? And He will help me? Are you sure?

"Why has no one told me this before? I've been confused for many years. Every time anyone talks to me about religion, I get the impression that they want to enlist me in their church or their denomination. But you! You've talked to me without *clichés* or religious bigotry. I have the feeling that there is hope for me, that Jesus is *The Way*, that the Gospel is put in true perspective, and that my life can now have purpose."

She left focused on a newly found life-pattern or model in the person of Jesus Christ. The New Testament would be her guide. Our books in French given to her by our translator would fortify the decision she had made to follow Jesus.

CHAPTER TEN

THE FATALISTIC PHOBIA

THE WHOLE WORLD is searching for purpose in life, for reality about God, for evidence that the Bible is true—and if so, how to make a practical application of it.

Society asks: Why is the cross of Christ so important and what does it mean? Why the constant guilt of sin and wrongdoing? What is the way to find peace with God? Can one find the right road?

Questions In The Quest

If God is good and if He created man and woman *in His own image*,^{Gen.1:26; 5:1-2} as the Bible says, why are the hearts and minds of many

56

people evil, full of hatred, jealousy, envy and murder?

If God is the Creator, what is the reason for so much poverty in this world? Why are there so many prayers without response from God? Why are there so many religions with so little right-eousness? Why is there so much knowledge with so few answers?

What causes loneliness, depression and suicide?

Why are there so many wars? Family disruption? Divorce? Violence? Brutality?

Why is it virtually impossible to keep the Ten Commandments?

Can what the Bible calls *Salvation* be a real, practical experience? Can a human person be re-born? Can one enjoy health, happiness, success and material blessings in this life?

Must one live in poverty in order to have true humility and be close to God? Can sickness and pain be the will of the Heavenly Father when earthly parents would never desire their children to be diseased?

Reject Religious Restraints

Religious tradition has programmed society to believe that God is enigmatic and mysterious. A limitation phobia prevents the majority of Christians from fulfilling the purpose God intends for them in life.

The business world believes in solving problems. But in the world of "religion" one may be counseled to ignore questions of logic and to continue a blindfolded march toward an uncertain future to face an ambiguous God, while committing one's life and circumstances to fate.

As a result, millions of people abandon their faith, relegating God, Jesus Christ and the Bible to primitive or medieval delusion and superstition.

It is time to reject religious limitations and see God as good, as big, as loving and as powerful as His Word says that He is.

O Lord God! Behold, You have made the heaven and the earth by Your power and stretched out arm, and there is nothing too hard for you.[Jer.32:17]

Chapter Eleven

Problems And Solutions At Their Source

WE HAVE BEEN privileged to proclaim the Good News of Jesus Christ to millions of people. Tens of thousands of lives have been lifted from despair to the discovery of new Life and peace.

Neither science, industry, religion nor philosophy can satisfy humanity's quest for God. When faith in Him is repudiated, people despair of faith in others and, consequently, no longer believe in themselves. They become apathetic and pursue life without meaningful purpose.

Without faith in God, people are psychologically vulnerable. They feed on philosophies that seem logical but that lead to emptiness and futility. Solomon said, *There is a way that seems right to people, but its end is the way of death.*[Pro.14:12]

Those who live in boredom and despondency may turn to lawlessness, destruction, murder and even suicide in their desperate search for something to fill the void in their lives.

With Modern Science
Is There Any Need For God?

Ecclesiastical orthodoxy has complicated the simplicity of God and His plan with a litany of religious rituals and incantations that offer little or no spiritual satisfaction.

A young Parisian collegiate asked, "Who needs God in our industrialized world of science?" Yet our most rudimentary problems remain unsolved.

A young businessman in London quipped, "Why do people cling to religion and believe in fables called *miracles*? Who needs them when we have the modern genius of medical science?" Yet many ordinary illnesses, such as the common cold, remain without a cure.

A young Brussels philosophy major ridiculed faith in God as she reasoned, "We enjoy the greatest psychological discoveries ever known. We are penetrating the complexities of the human mind until the ills of society can all be cured through the miracles of psychoanalysis." Yet there is a higher rate of suicide, per capita, today than ever before in human history.

The Toxin That Kills

People are at war within themselves. Emotional and psychological factors are destroying more human lives than at any time in history.

A psychiatrist at the world-famous Johns Hopkins Hospital reported that sixty percent of the patients there require mental and spiritual treatment, rather than physical.

It is estimated that fifty to eighty-five percent of people are passing on their mental and spiritual sicknesses to their bodies.

A management professional who takes over faltering businesses and gets them back on their feet estimates that ninety-five percent of the problems he encounters are not in the businesses but are in the persons who manage them.

People become disoriented in life and transmit their inner confusion to their business circumstances. They are perplexed or confused inside themselves and before long, their businesses reflect those maladies. When those managers are re-

THE MESSAGE THAT WORKS

oriented and re-stabilized on principles of biblical integrity and virtue, their business dilemmas are soon resolved.

Problems in marriages, in families, between neighbors, and in communities reside and smolder inside individuals.

Solve The Problem Begin At Home

When your own life is in order, your husband or wife, family or neighbors will be changed as though by a miracle. It is a psychological fact that what we think we hate in others is really what we despise in ourself—and, in fact, tend to impose upon others.

We can be jealous of only what we secretly desire to be or have or do. Jealousy is a self-confession of what we passionately envy.

The problem in one's home or family or job or neighborhood is the person one sees in the mirror. Get that person re-oriented and they will discover that they, alone, hold the power to re-shape their world. (Get my cassette series: *Faith To Change Your World.*)

This book is written to seed transformation inside the human spirit. It will happen as you read.

Chapter Twelve

Rising To A New Level

LEARN TO LIVE on the good side of life. One optimist said, "If you can't see the bright side of things, learn how to polish the dull side!"

There is no reason to live the life of a pessimist, lashing out at society and friends because the world you inhabit displeases you. God has provided for you, in seed-form, all that you can desire or need to reshape the world you live in.

Instead of being angry at society or relatives or friends, discover that God has created a paradise of blessing for you. Resolve to find *The Way* to God's rich blessings in life. The seven sections of this book, beginning at chapter fifteen, will lead you into God's fullness and blessing. Here is the essence of what we have told our world.

I. Dignity Restored

INSTEAD OF living with condemnation because of sin, discover that God has a plan to transfer to your account the righteousness and dignity of the greatest life ever lived—that of Jesus Christ.

II. Peace Recovered

INSTEAD OF living in torment with yourself and out of harmony with family and friends; instead of transferring mental anguish to your own body, your business, or your environment; instead of poisoning your own health and destroying your happiness, discover God's miracle plan that can change you. Let Him transfer His peace, tranquillity and harmony to you, making you His friend and partner.

III. Signals Refocused

INSTEAD OF existing in confusion, making wrong decisions, stumbling into failure and every conceivable trap of defeat, discover that God has a perfect and simple plan to give you direction and guidance in life so that you will enjoy success, blessing, and material abundance.

IV. Health Renewed

INSTEAD OF resigning yourself to disease and sickness, living vulnerable to the physical plagues that ravage human society, discover God's provision of abundant Life and miracle power to heal you not only of diseases, maladies and infirmities, but also to keep you and your house in health, physical fitness and long life.

V. Prosperity Regained

INSTEAD OF acquiescing to poverty and want; instead of considering yourself a victim of circumstances; instead of consenting to a hand-to-mouth existence, discover that God created all the wealth of this world to facilitate your blessing and His work. Embrace Him in partnership for Life and learn to appropriate His fullness.

VI. Friendship Resumed

INSTEAD OF surrendering to loneliness, discouragement and depression, discover that God wants to become your personal friend and that He wants to live at your house so that you can experience happiness, companionship and comfort with Him.

VII. Victory Retrieved

INSTEAD OF trying and failing in life, instead of accepting defeat, disappointment and frustration, never savoring the exhuberance of victory and success, make the glorious discovery that God is a winner, and when He is your intimate partner and friend in life, He wills that you always win the prize. Refuse to spend your days drinking the dregs of leftovers.

THINK AS BIG and as good as God is big and good. Think health, blessing, success, love and abundant living because this is God's redemptive plan for your life.

CHAPTER THIRTEEN

THE DECLINE
THE RECOVERY

ADAM AND EVE sinned against God in the beginning and allowed Satan to interdict their fellowship and communion, health and happiness, blessing and abundance with God.[Gen.3:]

Because God is righteous, He could not cohabit with sin, and He still cannot. Adam and Eve were banished from God's presence in the Garden of Eden [Gen.3:23-24] and were separated from Him by their sin.[Isa.59:2]

They subjugated themselves to Satan, their new master, when they believed his lying suggestion that God did not mean what He said.[Gen.3:1,4,6] Then followed the terrible consequences of sin which devastate human lives today.[Rom.5:12]

Humanity's Demoralization

1. Instead of forgiveness, there is hatred, malice, suspicion and judgment.

2. Instead of peace with God, there is unrest and guilt, inferiority and condemnation in the spirits of people.

3. Instead of the Lord's guidance and direction, there is delusion, deceit and perplexity.

4. Instead of health and energy, there is disease, sickness and physical suffering.

5. Instead of abundance, there is poverty, destitution and indigence.

6. Instead of God's presence, there is loneliness, estrangement, reclusion and even hostility.

7. Instead of achievement, there is disappointment, intimidation, defeat and enslavement.

God's *Redemptive* Solution

But *God so loved the world that He gave His only Son, that whoever believes in Him should not perish but have eternal life.*Joh. 3:16 NIV

Jesus said, *The thief (Satan) comes only to steal and kill and destroy; I have come that you may have life and that you may have it more abundantly.*Joh. 10:10 The Amplified Version of the Bible says: *that you may have and enjoy life, and have it in abundance — to the* *full, till it overflows.* God's redemptive plan is that we be the beneficiaries of all that He IS.

When Jesus Christ died in our place, He suffered the penalty that the law of eternal justice prescribed for you and me—Death! *The soul that sins shall die.*Eze.18:4,20 *The wages of sin is death.*Rom.6:23 Jesus Christ paid our fine for us when *He gave Himself a ransom for all* 1Ti.2:6 and when *we were reconciled to God by the death of His Son.* Rom.5:10

Christ's payment on our behalf was final. *We are sanctified through the offering of the body of Jesus Christ* **once for all**...*by one offering He perfected forever them that are sanctified...where remission of sin is, there is no more offering for sin.*Heb.10:10,14,18 Our sins and our transgressions have been punished in Christ. He suffered in our stead. He paid enough to reconcile us forever in God's sight.

Christ did it *For Us.*

We need never suffer again what He suffered in our place. He died as our substitute. We are forever free. That is the Good News. And when we believe it, God's power manifests the results of that Good News in our lives by miracles of His grace and love.

Through Christ's death on the cross in our stead, He paid the full price to provide for each of our seven basic needs. He *reconciled* us.2Co.5:18-19

CHAPTER FOURTEEN

PREVIEW OF REDEMPTIVE BLESSINGS

THE NEXT CHAPTER begins the seven sections of this book in which humanity's seven basic needs are expounded along with God's redemptive provisions for those seven needs. They are expressed so that as you read them, His power will take effect in your life—like a miracle, and actualize or manifest them.

All of God's blessings are provided for His children on a legal basis. I say "legal" because Christ gave His life to legally pay for them.

The number seven, according to Bible scholars, represents completeness and perfection. There are seven fundamental human needs. God's sevenfold nature and blessings are revealed by seven redemptive names. Christ's provision is sevenfold. Redemption is sevenfold.

What *"Redemptive"* Means

We call these seven provisions "redemptive" blessings because they are bought and paid for by the vicarious death, burial and resurrection of our Lord Jesus Christ. By that, we mean, He was our substitute who died, was buried and was raised from the dead in our name and on our behalf.

When we believe that, we are embracing the fact that our old life, our fallen, sinful nature, died and was buried with Christ so that now we can share His new, resurrection life. Paul said, *We are buried with him by baptism into death: that like as Christ was raised up from the dead by the Father, even so we should walk in newness of life.*^{Rom.6:4}

Christ sacrificed His own life, on our behalf, to ransom us from Satan's domain. By that we mean that His death paid the price for us to be bought back from the slavery of Satan, restored to God's family, and reconciled to Him. His life was given as a ransom that expunged our debt and restored us to the position with God that Adam and Eve had before they repudiated His Word and were enslaved by Satan. (Gen. chapters 1 & 2)

The Bible says of Christ: *You have redeemed us to God by your blood.*Rev.5:9 *You loved us, and washed us from our sins in your own blood.*Rev.1:5 *You purged us from our sins.*Heb.1:3 *The Son of man came...to give his life a ransom for many.* Mk.10:45

When Christ's work of redemption was accomplished on our behalf, *He sat down on the right hand of the Majesty on high.*Heb.1:3 Our redemption was a *fait accompli.* Now the benefits of that redemption are offered to us in the seeds of His living Word. Each seed is pregnant with His miracle Life and Power. Jesus said, *The words that I speak unto you are Spirit and Life.*Joh.6:63

By knowing God's promises, we know His will. It is always His will to do what He has promised. All persons of integrity *will* to fulfill their commitments. We know God's will by knowing His Word. That is why the Bible says, *Faith comes by hearing...the Word of God.*Rom.10:17

Rising To A New Level of *Life*

As you read the following seven sections of this book, you will become aware of God's seven provisions for your seven fundamental needs. When you *know these truths, they will make you free.* Joh.8:32 In other words, your life and circumstances will rise to the level of God's redemptive

72

plan and provisions. Faith will be born in you, creating new confidence in God's love for you.

This is the confidence that we have in Him, that, if we ask anything according to His will (or His Word of promise), He hears us: and if we know that He hears us, whatever we ask, we know that we have the petitions that we desired of Him.[1Joh.5:14-15]

Comprehending *Redemption*

The master key to receiving God's redemptive blessings is to realize that *they are each bought and paid for.* You can receive His blessings because Christ laid down His life to pay for them in your name.

I have elucidated God's seven redemptive provisions for you in the next seven sections of this book following the order noted in the distinguished Scofield Bible, page 7, item (4) under the commentary on Genesis 2:4. *Seven Redemptive Names of Jehovah.*

Section I. *DIGNITY RESTORED*

Jehovah-TSIDKENU, *God is our* RIGHTEOUS-NESS.[Jer.23:6]

Section II. *PEACE RECOVERED*

Jehovah-SHALOM, *God is our* PEACE.[Jdg.6:23-24]

Section III. *SIGNALS REFOCUSED*

Jehovah-RAAH, God is our GUIDE, our SHEP-HERD.[Psa.23:1]

Section IV. *HEALTH RENEWED*

Jehovah-RAPHA, God is our PHYSICIAN, our HEALER.[Exo.15:26]

Section V. *PROSPERITY REGAINED*

Jehovah-JIREH, God is our PROVIDER, our SOURCE.[Gen.22:8-14]

Section VI. *FRIENDSHIP RESUMED*

Jehovah-SHAMMAH, God is PRESENT.[Eze.48:35]

Section VII. *VICTORY RETRIEVED*

Jehovah-NISSI, God is our VICTORY.[Exo.17:15]

THIS MAY SOUND too theological to interest you, but let me explain something very simple that can be of great benefit in your life.

In the Old Testament, God revealed Himself to people through His Redemptive names. They identified His nature and unveiled what His plan of redemption would include in *the fullness of time.* ^{Gal.4:4; Eph.1:10} They became the identifiers or signals for redemptive faith in God.

On pages six and seven of the Scofield Bible, in his foot note on the redemptive names, Mr. Scofield said that the name "Jehovah is distinctly the redemptive name of Deity" and means "the self-existent One Who *reveals* Himself."

The Bible records many other names of Jehovah-God, but only seven *redemptive* ones, and they are never referred to except in His dealings with people. The notable F.F. Bosworth, author of the living classic book, *Christ The Healer,* points out, "There are not six redemptive names, or eight, but seven, the perfect number, because He is the perfect Savior and His redemption includes the perfect provision for every human need."

Mr. Bosworth adds, "In His redemptive relation to people, Jehovah has seven compound names which reveal Him as meeting every need of people…. Since it is His redemptive relation to us that these names reveal, they must each point to Calvary where we were redeemed."

Each of these seven redemptive names announces a special expression of God's nature and of His will for His children. Each blessing is provided by Christ's redemptive death on the cross. And that is the reason—the only reason—that you and I may receive them. *They are paid for.*

No More Ambiguity
Childhood Confidence

Without that understanding, faith may seem ambiguous. But with a grasp of this fact, faith becomes as uncomplicated as a child's confidence—which is the kind of faith that Christ commends. Mar.10:15 The simplicity of child-like faith is to perceive truth as a child does.

> You can have it if it is paid for. If God promised it, He wants to do it. Like any honest person, God wills to make His Word good. You can ask Him for anything that His Son died to pay for, and you can have confidence that you will receive it.

The facts of the Gospel are utterly simple. Religion has complicated them. Paul urged us to avoid being *corrupted from the simplicity that is in Christ.* 2Co.11:3

Before reading these seven sections that unveil God's seven redemptive blessings for your seven needs, here is a preview to seed you for a better comprehension of each provision.

DIGNITY RESTORED

1. THE NEED FOR *RIGHTEOUSNESS*.

Sin condemns us. We want God's forgiveness.

PROVISION: *The Lord* (is) *our righteousness*. [Jer.23:6] Jesus bore our sins on the cross; therefore, *the gift of righteousness* [Rom.5:17] is ours.

BASIS FOR FAITH: Christ was made sin with our sins and bore the punishment that we deserved.

PRAYER-CONFESSION: **Lord, you took my sins to the cross. Your blood was shed for their remission. I am restored to dignity with God.**

PEACE RECOVERED

2. THE NEED FOR *PEACE*.

God has forgiven us so we must forgive ourselves. We struggle adjusting to this New Life.

PROVISION: *The Lord is our peace.*[Jdg.6:20-24] Jesus *made peace through the blood of His cross.*[Col.1:20]

BASIS FOR FAITH: Christ endured our punishment in order to give us His peace.

PRAYER-CONFESSION: **Lord, you bore my judgment and made peace by the blood of the cross. My account was settled. I embrace your peace.**

✧ ✧ ✧

SIGNALS REFOCUSED

3. THE NEED FOR *GUIDANCE.*

We need direction in life to avoid deception, delusion and betrayal.

PROVISION: *The Lord is my shepherd.*[Psa.23:1] Jesus said, *My sheep hear my voice, and they follow me; a stranger they will not follow.*[Joh.10:27, 5]

BASIS FOR FAITH: Christ laid down His life to become our Good Shepherd so that we would never go, or be led astray.

PRAYER-CONFESSION: **Lord, I follow you. I know your voice. I cannot be misled when you are my guide.**

HEALTH RENEWED

4. THE NEED FOR *HEALING.*

Pain, disease, weakness and sickness ravage human society.

PROVISION: God says, *I am Lord who heals you;* or *I am the Lord your physician.*[Exo.15:26] He paid for our healing when He *took the stripes by which we were healed.*[Isa.53:4-5]

BASIS FOR FAITH: Christ suffered our diseases and bore them for us in His death so that we can have His Life, physically as well as spiritually.

PRAYER-CONFESSION: **Lord, you suffered my diseases for me so that I need never suffer them. My health is provided and I accept it now.**

✧ ✧ ✧

PROSPERITY REGAINED

5. THE NEED FOR *MATERIAL SUBSTANCE.*

Material privation, destitution, and indigence demoralizes humanity in the midst of a world of abundance.

PROVISION: *The Lord will provide.*[Gen.22:8] *My God shall supply all your needs according to His riches in glory by Christ Jesus.*[Phi.4:19]

BASIS FOR FAITH: Christ *became poor, that we, through His poverty, might be rich.*[2Co.8:9] He supplies all of our needs.

PRAYER-CONFESSION: **Lord, when you gave Jesus for me,** *you also freely gave me all things.* [Rom.8:32] **I claim what my present needs require.**

✧ ✧ ✧

FRIENDSHIP RESUMED

6. THE NEED FOR *GOD'S PRESENCE*.

Loneliness, reclusion and estrangement foster despair and hopelessness. We need a *friend who sticks closer than a brother or sister.*[Pro.18:24]

PROVISION: *The Lord is there* (or *present*) [Eze.48:35] because we were *made nigh by the blood of Christ.*[Eph.2:13]

BASIS FOR FAITH: Christ died to bring us back into God's household as members of His Family.

PRAYER-CONFESSION: **Lord, you expunged my sins that separated me from you. Now I am no longer alone.**

✧ ✧ ✧

VICTORY RETRIEVED

7. THE NEED FOR *VICTORY*.

Defeat, intimidation, fear and discouragement demean and deprecate people, interdicting success and achievement in life.

PROVISION: *The Lord (became) our banner* or *victor* or *captain* [Exo.17:15 LB] when Christ *triumphed over principalities and powers,*[Col.2:15] and *delivered us from darkness.*[Col.1:13]

BASIS FOR FAITH: Christ died to *destroy all the works of the devil.*[1Jo.3:8] He now becomes our victory and unfurls His banner over our lives.

PRAYER-CONFESSION: **Lord, you removed Satan's authority over my life and translated me into your kingdom.** *If God be for me, who can be against me?* [Ro.8:31] **Now I share your victory.**

NOW WE ARE READY to examine the divine impact of God's seven redemptive provisions for our lives. As you comprehend each of these seven significant truths, it will bring a new exhiliration and spiritual stamina into your life. Do not *try* to make that happen. Just read and learn and *let* each new discovery procreate itself in your life. The fundamental, biblical truths that you are about to read are, in essence, the facts that undergird *The MESSAGE That WORKS.*

THE MESSAGE THAT WORKS

Section I

Dignity Restored

✧ 📖 ✧

RIGHTEOUSNESS RENEWED

GOD REVEALS HIMSELF BY HIS *REDEMPTIVE* NAME, *JEHOVAH-TSIDKENU*, TRANSLATED *"THE LORD OUR RIGHTEOUSNESS."* JER.23:6 FORGIVENESS IS A *REDEMPTIVE* BLESSING, PAID FOR ON OUR BEHALF AND IN OUR NAME WHEN *"JESUS CHRIST HIS OWN SELF BORE OUR SINS IN HIS OWN BODY ON THE TREE,"* 1PE.2:24 OPENING THE WAY FOR EVERY PERSON TO RECEIVE *"THE GIFT OF RIGHTEOUSNESS."* ROM.5:17

CHAPTER FIFTEEN

THE REMEDY FOR GUILT

EVERY MAN AND every woman needs God's righteousness and forgiveness. Since the original sin in the Garden of Eden,^{Gen.3:} the divine dignity that Adam and Eve were created with was compromised, and could never be recovered *until Jesus gave His life for us when we were brought back to God...as His friends (so that now) He is living within us again.*^{Rom.5:10 LB}

Unless Christ has saved you, the sins you have committed against God, and His laws that you have broken, are factors that predetermine your final judgment and condemnation.

People's sense of guilt and unworthiness before God causes them to feel inadequate to pray and unworthy of receiving answers.

Indignity And Ignominy

Sin-consciousness destroys faith in God, in the Bible, in others and most of all, in one's self. This sense of inadequacy discourages initiative. It engenders an inferiority complex. One becomes snared by negativism and lives with a sense of condemnation, in fear of God, searching for someone else to pray for them because of their own sense of indignity and ignominy before God.

In their vain search to find peace, people try church attendance, benevolence, penance, prayers, fasting, confessions, good works, abstention from pleasures and bad habits, self-denial, pilgrimages, even flagellation and other forms of self-inflicted punishment.

But this search never ends because, being created *in the image of God – in His likeness,*^{Gen.1:27; 5:1-2} each human person is made to walk with Him and to fellowship with Him, like Adam and Eve did in the Garden of Eden. People were created for God's righteousness, to share His nature and to express His dignity. When sin entered the human race, righteousness was forfeited and the human species has been lost and bewildered.

The Way Of Recovery

To regain this sense of righteousness is the reason for religions—non-Christian ones as well as those of the cultured and industrialized worlds. (When I speak of *religions*, I mean rituals and ceremonies without Life.)

God has provided *The Way* for us to rediscover what was lost in the Garden of Eden. He has given us the power to become His children ^{Joh. 1:12} with all of the privileges of being re-born into His Royal Family.

But the tormenting consciousness of sin, guilt and unworthiness persists as long as we remain uninformed about God's plan of Salvation. (Get my book, *God's Love Plan*.)

Christ gave His life to bear the penalty of our sins. We can receive God's righteousness and stand once again in His presence without the consciousness of sin, guilt, fear or inferiority. That is what humanity craves. This haunting sin and guilt complex must be expunged. God's righteousness is the only answer.

Chapter Sixteen

Free Again

THE BIBLE SAYS: *The Lord [is] our righteousness.* Jer.23:6 It teaches that our sins have been put to the account of Jesus, and now His righteousness has been credited to our account.2Co.5:21

The Living Bible says: *For God took the sinless Christ and poured into Him our sins. Then, in exchange, He poured God's goodness into us.*2Co.5:21 LB

*Being justified freely by His grace through the redemption that is in Christ Jesus whom God set forth to be a propitiation [effecting reconciliation] through faith in His blood, to declare His righteousness for the remission of our sins.*Rom.3:24-25

Many people wonder how this is possible.

Good News—Restoration

God has provided for our restoration to Him. We can regain the personal relationship with Him that was abrogated when Adam and Eve disobeyed His Word. The price has been paid for the restoration of our own human dignity. It is all summed up in the word *righteousness.*

The message of the Gospel is that God has charged our sins to Christ's account, and has now credited His righteousness to our account.[2Co.5:21] Consequently, we can stand in God's presence with all the legal rights of a Royal Family Member—a child of God.[Joh. 1:12]

The Living Bible says: *God showed His great love by sending Christ to die for us while we were still sinners...and now He has declared us not guilty.... Since, when we were His enemies, we were brought back to God by the death of His Son, what blessings He must have for us now that we are His friends and He is living within us! Now we rejoice in our wonderful new relationship with God—all because of what our Lord Jesus Christ has done in dying for our sins—making us friends of God.*[Rom.5:8-11 LB]

Peter wrote: *Who His own self bare our sins in His own body on the tree, that we, being dead to sins, should live unto righteousness.*[1Pe.2:24]

Debts Can Only Be Paid Once

Since no debt can be paid twice nor can anyone be legally punished twice for the same crime, when Jesus suffered the sentence of our sins, we were forever absolved.[Mat. 26:28 Heb. 10:18]

With no sins laid to our charge, there is no more record of our iniquities that separated us from God.[Rev.1:5] He welcomes us back into His presence [Eph.2:13] and imparts to us His own righteousness. [Rom.3:22-26 1Co.1:30]

We can now live in God's Holy Presence as Adam and Eve did before they sinned. All we have to do is believe this Good News and confess our faith before God and before people [Rom.10:9-10] by our words and by our actions.[1Co.1:18,21]

That is the message of the Gospel. All we need to do is *only believe*.[Mar.5:36; Rom.1:16] Believe what? Believe what the Bible says.

God made Him [Christ] to be sin for us, who knew no sin; that we might be made the righteousness of God in Him.[2Co.5:21]

The Lord [is] our righteousness.[Jer.23:6]

In God's Presence Without
Fear, Guilt Or Inferiority

Jesus became our righteousness by bearing our sins on the Cross; therefore, *the gift of righteousness* now belongs to us.[Rom.5:17] He paid for it.

Our sins can no longer condemn us because Christ has put them away forever. The penalty of our transgressions against God has been suffered. [1Pe.2:24] The payment has been made. You and I are now free—forever![Rom.6:18,22] *Only believe!*

God offers us His righteousness.[Rom.3:25-26] We can enjoy the privilege of standing in His presence without the consciousness of sin, fear, guilt, or inferiority.[Rom.8:32-34]

OUR DIVINE DIGNITY IS RESTORED.

Chapter Seventeen

The Prayer-Confession

WHEN GOD GAVE His Son and when Jesus gave His life to ransom us from the dominion of Satan, that was the proof that God loves us and wants to share His Life with us.

That is the only basis on which we can approach God, knowing that His pardon has been granted and that He wills to impart to us His own righteousness as soon as we believe.

Knowing this, you can come before Him right now. Pray this prayer speaking each word aloud from your heart:

DEAR LORD: I have sinned against you. I was condemned to eternal death by your Law,

because your Word says *the soul that sins shall die* Eze.18:20 and the w*ages of sin is death.*Rom.6:23

Because I was condemned by my sins,Joh.3:18 I was separated from your presence.Isa.59:2 I could not approach you without this terrible sense of guilt.

But now I understand that Jesus died in my place, suffering the judgment of all of my sins. 1Pe.2:24 He paid for my rebellion. The wages of my sins was death — and Jesus died as my substitute.

I KNOW THAT NO CRIME can be punished twice. When a debt is paid, it cannot be paid a second time. It no longer exists.

Since Jesus Christ suffered in my place, there is no more punishment for me to bear, and my debt no longer exists.Rom.8:1

You now give to me your own righteousness. 1Co.1:30 I accept Jesus Christ now. This is a miracle. I accept your gift of Life and righteousness. Rom.5:17-18

NOW I HAVE JESUS Christ in me.Gal.2:20 I can now stand in your presence without the consciousness of sin, guilt, fear, or inferiority, because I am your child.Joh.1:12 You are my Father.Gal.4:6

Your righteousness is mine. I am re-born. I can walk and live with the *dignity* that you created me for.

Thank you Lord. My divine DIGNITY IS RESTORED. Amen!

SECTION I — DIGNITY RESTORED

Section II

Peace Recovered

✧ 📖 ✧

PEACE WITH GOD

GOD REVEALS HIMSELF BY HIS *REDEMPTIVE* NAME, *JEHOVAH-SHALOM*, TRANSLATED *"THE LORD OUR PEACE."* [JDG.6:20-24] GOD'S PEACE IS A *REDEMPTIVE* BLESSING, PAID FOR ON OUR BEHALF AND IN OUR NAME WHEN *"THE CHASTISEMENT OF OUR PEACE WAS UPON HIM"* [ISA.53:5] AND HE *"MADE PEACE THROUGH THE BLOOD OF HIS CROSS"* [COL.1:20] FOR EVERYONE WHO BELIEVES.

✧ ✧

CHAPTER EIGHTEEN

INNER CONFLICT

IN SECTION ONE, we showed how God's righteousness replaces human guilt and restores Divine Dignity. The result is *peace with God through our Lord Jesus Christ.*Rom.5:1

When the Savior was born, angels announced, *Peace and good will toward people.*Luk.2:14 The mission of our Lord to this world was to bring peace.

This section emphasizes why people need this peace, how God identifies Himself as *the God of peace* Rom.15:33 by one of His redemptive names, and why His peace can be embraced now.

Peace and harmony are part of God's nature. He created man and woman to share His rich life of love and gentleness. But sin entered the human race. Its evil seed produced violence, unrest, rebellion, fear, hatred and death.

The Troubled Sea

Unless we have been born again, embracing the righteousness of God by faith, the harmony between people and Him that was disrupted in the Garden of Eden cannot be experienced. Human nature is *like the troubled sea, when it cannot rest, whose waters cast up mire and dirt. There is no **peace**, says my God, to the wicked.*[Isa.57:20-21]

Void of God's peace, society is depraved and perverted by destructive influences. Fear torments people, demoralizing them and diminishing their potential.

Harmony with God is the only thing that can dispel the turmoil and assuage the conflict that prevails in the human spirit that is out of tune with its Creator.

People may seek to alleviate fears and insecurity with education, philosophy, religion, pleasures, entertainment and sensuality.

But without communion with God, there can never be peace and the search will never end.

Wars, family discord, community violence, insane acts of brutality, hatred, abuse and murder are all due to the lack of peace with God in the human heart.

Disease, tension, emotional conflict, bitterness, shame, physical deterioration and suffering are rooted in people's lack of peace with God.

Peace With *God*—With *Ourselves*

When we are not at peace with God, we are not at peace with our nation, with our neighbors, with our family — or even with ourselves.

Jesus said: *From within, out of the heart of a person, proceed evil thoughts, adulteries, fornication, murders, thefts, covetousness, wickedness, deceit, lasciviousness, an evil eye, blasphemy, pride, foolishness: All these evil things come from within, and defile the person.*[Mar.7:21-23]

But once peace is born in the human heart, it is the most powerful force for healing and harmony, for love and kindness, and for success and achievement in this world.

CHAPTER NINETEEN

EXONERATED

GOD ANNOUNCES, *Behold, I give my covenant of peace.*[Num.25:12] Paul says of Christ, *He is our peace.*[Eph.2:14] Jesus said, *My peace I give unto you.*[Joh.14:27]

God's will for humanity in this turbulent world is an abundance of His peace. He is *the God of peace.*[Rom.15:33]

The Meaning of *PEACE*

The Bible meaning of *peace* in both Hebrew and Greek is to be well, happy, healthy, prosperous, restful, safe, whole, secure, quiet and set at one again with God. This is the glorious and harmonious state of being which He created you and me to experience.

When humankind transgressed God's Law, they could not remain in fellowship with Him and were therefore expelled from His presence to become subjugated by Satan and to live under the dominion of death. In this fallen state of banishment from God, there could be no peace.

But God, who loved us so much that He was *not willing that any should perish*,[2Pe.3:9] made a way for us to be ransomed from the slavery of Satan and restored to the position for which He created us, so that His peace could once again reign in our hearts.

He sacrificed *His only begotten Son* [Joh.3:16] who took upon himself our sins and transgressions [1Pe.2:24] that had separated us from God. [Isa.59:2]

Our Substitute

Jesus committed no sin; instead He assumed the guilt of our sins.[2Co.5:21] He made himself accountable for our transgressions then endured the penalty of our sins so that nothing could be laid to our charge.[Rom.8:33] *Christ's death on the Cross made **peace** with God for all by His blood.*[Col.1:20 LB]

He declared us *not guilty* any more. He exonerated us.[Rom.5:9 LB] *He freely took away our sins and gave us His glorious Life instead.*[Rom.5:16 LB]

That message is what the Bible calls *the Gospel of **peace*** [Rom.10:15] and we are encouraged to tell it to the whole world.[Isa.61:1; Mar.16:15; 1Co.15:1-2]

It is the message that my wife and I have announced in nearly eighty nations during over a half century. It is *The MESSAGE That WORKS*. Knowing this, one suddenly realizes that there is no more enmity between one's self and God. Eph.2:15-16

Peace And Restoration

As this truth dawns and as people embrace Christ as their Lord and Savior, He actually comes into their lives.Col.1:27; Gal.2:20 His peace becomes their peace. His Life becomes theirs. The Prince of Peace reigns inside them and they are restored to Him. Jesus becomes their Lord.2Co.6:18

All of this is the work of God's grace. No one can merit it. It was God who initiated the work of redemption on our behalf. He believed that if people knew the price His Son paid for their salvation, that they would respond and would be as eager to be at peace with Him as He is to have them near Him.

Now these Bible verses will be meaningful.

*In Christ Jesus, you who sometimes were far off are made near by the blood of Christ. For He is our **peace**. Having abolished in His flesh the enmity [between God and people), so making **peace**, that He might reconcile both to God…by the Cross.*Eph.2:13-16

*The punishment for our **peace** was upon Him* [Isa.53:5] when *He made **peace** through the blood of His Cross…to present you holy and unblamable and unre-provable in His sight.*[Col.1:19-20,22]

No longer do we need to fear judgement for our past sins. Jesus suffered our penalty. Our past is like a debt that has been paid. It is expunged from the record. This is salvation, the truth that brings peace.

Unblameable Unreproveable

The record of our past sins no longer exists to condemn us. *Jesus made **peace** by the blood of His Cross.*[Col.1:19-20,22] Our account has been expunged. The law of sin and evil can no longer dominate us when we are restored to God. He is now our peace.

Peace Is Recovered

When a great man of God in the Bible met an angel face to face, the Lord said, *Peace be unto you, fear not.… Then Gideon built an altar there to the Lord and called it Jehovah-**shalom**, which means, The Lord is our **peace**.*[Jdg.6:23-24]

When the heavenly host announced the birth of Jesus, the message was: *Glory to God in the highest, and on earth **peace**, good will toward all people.*[Luk.2:14]

Jesus said: *Peace I leave with you, My **peace** I give to you...so let not your heart be troubled, neither let it be afraid.*[Joh.14:27] *He is our **peace**.*[Eph.2:14]

That is why our ministry consists of *preaching (or teaching or telling of) **peace** by Jesus Christ,*[Acs.10:36] because people can only know peace by knowing what Jesus did for them and by knowing the price that He paid to give them His peace.

*Therefore being justified by faith, we have **peace** with God through our Lord Jesus Christ.*[Rom.5:1]

PEACE IS NOW RECOVERED.

CHAPTER TWENTY

THE PRAYER-
CONFESSION

KNOWING THAT CHRIST has redeemed you from the dominion of sin, make your prayer a confession of embracing Him and His peace.

Remember that the only reason anyone can receive God's peace and be delivered from condemnation, insecurity and fear, is that Jesus Christ bore the punishment for our peace [Isa.53:5] so that we can now stand in God's presence unblamable and unreproveable. Say this, aloud to Him:

DEAR LORD: I confess that without you, I was tormented by fear and condemnation. My world was a restless ocean of disharmony.

I know that *all have sinned and come short of the glory of God,* and that *there is no peace... to the wicked.*[Isa.57:21]

Now I have discovered *the Gospel of peace.* I know that my transgressions have been punished and my penalty has been paid by Jesus Christ, on my behalf and in my name. The punishment I ought to have suffered was endured by Him because He became accountable for me.

I needed to be at peace with *you* so that I can be at peace with *myself,* my *family,* my *neighbors* and my *world.*

O LORD, what a miracle of grace that my sins have been abolished through the blood of Jesus Christ. My account is paid in full. I am redeemed.

You and I are *at peace* now. The conflict ended at the Cross. I can now stand in your presence without condemnation. My death and judgment are past. My debt is paid. I am saved. I am reconciled to you.

I can now enjoy the lifestyle that you provided for me. *PEACE IS RECOVERED.* Amen!

Section III

Signals Refocused

✧ 📖 ✧

GUIDANCE
IS NOW AVAILABLE

GOD REVEALS HIMSELF BY HIS *REDEMPTIVE* NAME, *JEHOVAH-RA-AH*, TRANSLATED *"THE LORD IS MY SHEPHERD."* PSA.23:1 GUIDANCE IS A *REDEMPTIVE* BLESSING, PAID FOR ON OUR BEHALF AND IN OUR NAME WHEN JESUS CHRIST *"LAID DOWN HIS LIFE FOR THE SHEEP,"* JOH.10:14-15 TO REDEEM US TO HIMSELF AS OUR GUIDE AND SHEPHERD.

◇ ◇

Chapter Twenty-One

The Bitter Cup

IN THE FIRST two sections of this book, we showed you *The Way* back to God, and how to have His dignity and peace restored in life.

In this section, you will discover how to be guided and directed by your Lord so that you will escape the confusion and instability that plague and divert so many lives.

To succeed, you must make right decisions. The Bible says, *The Lord will guide you continually.* [Isa.58:11] *God will guide you with His counsel.* [Psa.73:24]

God's Rhythm Is Beautiful

You and I were created to know God, to fit into His divine plan, to accomplish His design. [Gen.1:28] Like the orbit of the stars or the rhythm of the seasons, God's plan for each life is beautiful and perfect. [Jas.1:17]

But after Adam and Eve disobeyed God in the Garden of Eden, sin dominated their lives and the lives of their descendants. People became subservient to another master, Satan.

Every good, pure, beautiful and successful design for life became ambiguous. Motives became devious; objectives, distorted. Direction was lost and guidance was confused.^{Rom.1:21; Jer.50:6; Lam.4:14; Mat.13:14-15; Acs.28:27; Eph.4:18-19}

Pathways Became Pitfalls

Human hearts were menaced by terror. Dreams were shattered. Happiness and success became elusive. There was endless struggle instead of fulfillment, drudgery instead of pleasure. Every lifestream was stained by crime. The air was corrupted. The cup of life became bitter. Life's pathways were filled with pitfalls and danger. People lost their way.^{Psa.53:5; Isa.53:6; Rom.3:23}

Achievement and success were subverted. Understanding was obscured. Confidence was broken. Where velvet was promised, there was a shroud. Bondage instead of liberty became the master. Gall instead of nectar became life's portion. Sackcloth took the place of silk.^{Isa.1:4-6; Jer.8:22; 30:12-13}

Chapter Twenty-Two

No More Separation

IN THIS LABYRINTH of human disillusionment, people desperately needed to recover
God's direction for life. His ideals are construc-
tive. His motives are pure and loving.^{Psa. 19:7-9}

But ever since the fall of human nature, a vi-
cious driving-force has hurled people into the
turbulent stream of insecurity. It has catapulted
them over the precipice into utter darkness and
separation from God.

*All we like sheep have gone astray; we have turned
everyone to his or her own way.*^{Isa.53:6}

Lost Signals—Human Trauma

With divine signals scrambled or lost because of the crafty Deceiver, humanity experienced the traumatic dilemma that Solomon wrote about: *There is a way that seems right to people, but in the end it leads to death.*[Pro.14:12; 16:25]

The Bible says that because people have uncertain goals and confused motives, they *are tempted, when drawn away by their own lust, and enticed. Then when lust has conceived, it brings forth sin; and sin, when it is finished, brings forth death.*[Jam.1:14-15]

Because the curtain of sin separates people from God, His signals cannot direct the course of their journey. They miss the road; they crash the reef; they drift off course; they sheer the bridge; they hit the mines. Every worthwhile dream sooner or later fades into an empty mirage.

They need God's direction—His divine guidance for true fulfillment in life.

Chapter Twenty-Three

Delivered From Deception

THE PSALMIST DAVID said, *The Lord is my Shepherd.*[Psa.23:1]

It is God's desire to direct the details of your life so that you can enjoy the fruitful and rewarding experiences of success and happiness.

Jesus said, *I am the good shepherd, and I know my sheep.*[Joh.10:14] He said, *the good shepherd gives His life for the sheep.*[Joh.10:11]

Jesus became your shepherd and guide by giving His life for you. He died for you in order to abolish forever your sins which separated you from God. Now He wants to show you *The Way* to real living.

113

The Crafty Plunderer

People have lost their way because of sin in fallen human nature. Rebellion against God opened the way for Satan to subjugate people, misguiding them with all that is deceptive, crafty and illusory. Being separated from God by sin, confusion and delusion have supplanted His divine leadership and direction.

We Were Never Left To Drift

But God loved us too much to leave us adrift at sea without a compass. He sent His Son to die in our place so that we could find *The Way* back into His family.

His Word says, *Your iniquities have separated between you and your God,*[Isa.59:2] but Jesus broke down *the middle wall of partition between us and God*[Eph.2:14] by *bearing our sins in His own body on the tree.*[1Pe.2:24] *His blood was shed for the remission of sins*[Mat.26:28] and now *sin shall not have dominion over us who believe*[Rom.6:14] because we have been *made free from sin.*[Rom.6:18]

Now the signals between us and our Good Shepherd are refocused. We are retuned, reconnected, re-aligned with our Creator. Once again our communications are clear. The static and interference have been eliminated. Our rapport with Him is no longer obstructed by friction or conflict.

With *our sins washed away through the blood of Christ,*[Col.1:14,20] there is *nothing more to separate us from God.*[Eph.1:7; Lev.17:11; Heb.9:22; 10:18]

The Good Shepherd gave His Life for the sheep. He said, *I am the Way, the Truth and the Life: no one comes to the Father, but by me.*[Joh.14:6] He is *The Way* There is no deceit in Him.[1Pe.2:22]

Chapter Twenty-Four

Your New Guide

WHEN JESUS CHRIST endured the punishment for the sins of humanity, our debt was paid in full. This ended Satan's authority over us. Eph.1:20-22; Rom.5:17

Satan no longer has the right to confuse, deceive and misguide us.[Rom.6:14] Once we give Christ the reins of our life, our enemy no longer has the right to distort our guidance signals.[Rom.6:22] Our Shepherd takes control.[Joh.10:27-28] We no longer need to be vulnerable to the enemy's delusions. Jesus died to tear down the wall of separation between us and God.[Eph.2:13-14] Now we are restored to Him. We know *The Way*. We follow our Shepherd. Our signals are refocused.

The Good Shepherd In Charge

Before receiving Christ, we served a lying, crafty and insidious slave-driver. But when Christ becomes our Lord, we yield our guidance system to our Good Shepherd. He is given charge of our lives and the signals between us are no longer distorted.

He makes us to lie down in green pastures.

We fear no evil.

He prepares a table before us in the presence of our enemies.

Our cup overflows.

Surely goodness and mercy shall follow us all the days of our life.[Psa.23:2,4,5,6]

CHAPTER TWENTY-FIVE

STAYING ON COURSE

No ONE WAS MADE to walk life's pathway alone. There are perilous mountains scarred by deep ravines and gulches. There are rampaging rivers, avalanches, slides, enemies, storms and hazards.

But the Good Shepherd knows every pitfall. When He takes charge of our lives, we can confess with David, *The Lord shall preserve me from all evil.*[Psa.121:7]

Our dreams will know fulfillment. Our road will be lighted all the way when we walk with God and trust His direction as our Shepherd.

The Lord shall guide you continually.[Isa.58:11]

The steps of a good man or woman are ordered by the Lord.^{Psa.37:23}

Your Word is a lamp unto my feet, and a light unto my path.^{Ps. 119:105}

The Lord is my shepherd.^{Psa.23:1}

Jesus said, *My sheep hear my voice...and they follow me;*^{Joh.10:27} *a stranger will they not follow.*^{Joh.10:5}

Built-In Guidance System

With Jesus Christ living in you, you have a built-in guidance system that is reliable. He paid for the privilege of leading you. He gave *His life for the sheep.*^{Joh.10:11}

God wills that you have distinct, clear guidance so that you can discover and enjoy His best. The enemy has no further right to confuse and deceive you. Believe that the Lord is guiding you.

You have welcomed Him into your life. Yield to Him full control. YOUR SIGNALS ARE NOW REFOCUSED.

Chapter Twenty-Six

The Prayer-Confession

HAVING REALIZED THAT the Good Shepherd gave His life to ransom you from the jurisdiction of Satan, expect Him to give you guidance in every decision of life that you make.

Confess this to Him aloud and reverently:

> **DEAR LORD: Before I knew how you gave your life in order to direct me in life, I was misguided and adrift without a rudder.**
>
> **Hopes became disappointments. Ambitions ended in failures. Instead of joy, there was unhappiness, boredom instead of fulfillment.**
>
> **Promises were broken. Dreams were shattered. Storms clouded my skies. Accomplishments eluded me.**

My signals were coming from the wrong source. My decisions were miscalculated because I was on the wrong wave length.

BUT YOU SAW ME bewildered and confused. You cared for me enough to shine your light on my pathway to guide me back to you.

You saw how I served the designs of Satan, chasing his rainbows, misguided by his craftiness. Your signals of love could not reach me because my sins had raised a wall of separation between us.

I THANK YOU, DEAR LORD. You paid the price for my rebellion. You made yourself an offering for my sins.[Isa.53:10; Eph.5:2; Heb.10:10] You became my sacrifice—*the Lamb of God that takes away the sins of the world*[Joh.1:29] You bore the punishment for my sins.[Isa.53:5-6] You proved how much you wanted to guide and direct me toward happiness, peace, health and fulfillment.

NOW MY LIFE IS YOURS. You are at the helm of my ship. You will *guide my feet into the way of peace.*[Luk.1:79] Your Spirit will *guide me into all truth.*[Joh.16:13]

Now I can truly enjoy the redemptive blessing of living a life that is guided by you to fulfill your plan. My *SIGNALS ARE REFOCUSED.* Amen!

SECTION III — SIGNALS REFOCUSED

Section IV

Health
Renewed

✧ 📖 ✧

THE GREAT PHYSICIAN
PHYSICAL HEALTH

GOD REVEALS HIMSELF BY HIS *REDEMPTIVE* NAME, *JEHOVA-RAPHA,* TRANSLATED *"I AM THE LORD THAT HEALETH THEE"* OR *"I AM THE LORD YOUR PHYSICIAN. "*Exo.15:26 PHYSICAL HEALING IS A *REDEMPTIVE* BLESSING, PAID FOR ON OUR BEHALF AND IN OUR NAME WHEN JESUS CHRIST *"HIMSELF TOOK OUR INFIRMITIES AND BARE OUR SICKNESSES"* Mat.8:17 SO THAT THERE COULD NEVER BE A DOUBT ABOUT HIS WILL TO HEAL US.

◇ ◇

Chapter Twenty-Seven

No Longer Victimized

ONE OF THE MOST urgent human needs is for physical health. In human society, minds are distorted, disease and suffering are rampant, despondency and disillusionment reigns, hospitals are over-run. Psychiatrists and psychologists are often as bewildered as their patients are.

A great majority of people psychologically transmit their spiritual and mental problems to their physical bodies so that, in spite of the achievements of medical science, they become incurable from a human point of view.

The Source Of Sickness

You may be in need of physical health, facing the possibility of an incurable illness. Many people think it is normal to live subject to disease and suffering. They never question the source of this menacing dilemma. If a symptom appears, they rush to their doctor, then to their pharmacist with foreboding apprehension.

Many assume that God may be using sickness for some mysterious purpose in their lives. Or they may think that it can teach them some lesson in patience, humility, endurance or submission.

God provides physical health for you so that you can be at your best for *Him*, for *others* and for *yourself*. You need good health to be able to realize accomplishments, to fulfill your duties and desires in life among your family, in your neighborhood, in your business and in your world.

Is It God—Or Fate?

There is a power greater than disease. God has bestowed His healing love upon all who embrace Him as Savior. Be receptive to the Great Physician who will come to you as He has to multitudes worldwide.

The truths of healing expressed in this section can be as alive as God is because *His Words are Spirit and they are Life.*[Joh.6:63]

As we have proclaimed the truths of God's healing love worldwide, tens of thousands of sick and suffering people have been miraculously healed while listening. Jesus said, *the truth will make you free.*[Joh.8:32]

We did not know about their cases any more than we know about yours. We did not lay our hands on them and pray for them individually any more than I can lay my hands on you and pray for you now. They simply heard and believed, and God made His Word good in their lives. That can happen to you as you continue reading these pages.

Chapter Twenty-Eight

The Destructive Decline

GOD CREATED Adam and Eve perfect, physically, mentally, spiritually, and He placed them in the Garden of Eden amidst His abundance. They were not sick or incapacitated by disease.

God's plan for those whom He created *in His own image* Gen.1:26-27; 5:1-2 could never have included disease and infirmity. If He had designed them for pain and malady, would He have created them in such perfection?

God's message is about showing you *The Way* back to the paradise enjoyed before Adam and Eve sinned. His plan for humanity has never changed. He wills His best for all who believe.

Did God Mean What He Said?

Satan, the tempter, persuaded Adam and Eve to doubt God's Word. The cunning question that he posed to them was: *Has God said?*[Gen.3:1]

They concluded that God did not mean what He said when He warned: *Of the tree of the knowledge of good and evil, you shall **not** eat of it: for in the day that you eat it you shall surely **die**.*[Ge.2:17] They disobeyed the Lord, and were consequently banished from the paradise that He had created for them, and they began to die.

From that day, Adam and Eve became subjugated by Satan and their descendants exhibited the sad results of doubting God's Word. All that was perfect in them began to deteriorate. That process continues today. With every sin committed, something dies in the one who sins.

Subversion Of Faith

Happiness degenerates into sadness; love, into hatred. Life is plagued by disease and eventual death. Beauty turns to ashes. Faith is subverted by distrust, and confidence is displaced by deception. Healthy bodies become subject to the destructive power and influence of Satan who *came to steal and kill and destroy.*[Joh.10:10]

God Has Not Abandoned Us

The twin evils, sin and sickness, have marched hand-in-hand throughout all generations since Adam and Eve. The human mind and heart have degenerated through sin and corruption.

In spite of the prodigious achievements of modern science, incurable diseases still threaten human society.

Is there an answer? Has God abandoned us to this plight? Is physical healing part of His redemptive plan for humanity?

CHAPTER TWENTY-NINE

THE HEALER

GOD ANNOUNCES, *I am the Lord who heals you*.[Exo. 15:26] or, *I am the Lord your physician.*

You may find it difficult to reconcile this with so much sickness in our world, with so many innocent people suffering, and with so much negative religious teaching about disease.

If you are cognizant of God's redemptive plan for humanity, you will know that His will is for you to have physical health as well as spiritual salvation and material blessings.

John wrote, *I wish above all things that you may prosper (be helped, to succeed in affairs) and be in* **health**, *even as your soul prospers.*[3Jo.2]

When Jesus Christ died on the Cross, the Bible says that He bore our physical diseases in the same way that He bore our sins and our iniquities. So the question is not: Did He bear our physical diseases? The question is: Why?

The same verb in both Hebrew and Greek that is used to state that Jesus Christ bore our spiritual iniquities is also used to state that He bore our physical diseases.[Isa.53:4-5; Mat.8:16-17; 1Pe.2:24]

Christ's Vicarious Intervention

Why did Christ bear them? The answer constitutes the essence of Good News to those who are physically ill. He did it so that you do not have to do it. He did it as your personal substitute. That is why you can be healed.

He bore your diseases so that *the Life also of Jesus might be made manifest in your mortal flesh, or bodies.* 2Co.4:10

That is *The MESSAGE That WORKS.*

CHAPTER THIRTY

SICKNESS WAS NEVER GOD'S PLAN

IT WAS NEVER God's plan for His people to be sick and weak or to suffer pain and disease.

The plague of physical disease came about after Adam and Eve bowed to Satan's temptation. *Sin was conceived. And when it was finished, it brought forth death.*[Jam.1:15]

This beautiful couple whom God created *in His own image and likeness* [Gen.1:26-27; 5:1-2] had to be banished from His presence because He cannot co-exist or cohabit with sin. The seeds of sin produced their harvest and humanity began to deteriorate and die.

The wickedness of people was great in the earth, and every imagination of the thoughts of their hearts were only evil continually.[Gen.6:5-6] The lifestyle of people deteriorated into a veritable breeding ground for disease and decay. Disharmony and deceit, jealousy and hatred, envy and lust, violence and murder poisoned every fiber of the human spirit and that poison invaded the physical body too.

God Planned "Redemption"

Deuteronomy, Chapter 28, outlines the destructive harvest of disobedience to God. It enumerates a forbidding litany of physical diseases which humankind suffers: *Pestilence, vexation, comsumption, fever, inflammation, extreme burning, mildew, the botch of Egypt, emerods, scab, itch, madness, blindness, astonishment of heart, oppression, violence, smiting in the knees and in the legs, sore botch, hunger, thirst, nakedness, want of all things, distress, plagues, sicknesses [and so much more].*[Deu.28:15,20-22,27-29,35,60-61,65-67]

Then a comprehensive footnote is added to the gruesome catalog: *Also every sickness and every plague which is not written in the book of this law.*[v.61]

But God, who is Love and Life—God who created man and woman *in His own image* [Gen.1:26-27; 5:1-2]—could not abandon His dream.

As Adam and Eve left His presence to be subjugated by Satan's scourge of depravity and despair, God was conceiving His plan of redemption to bring them back into His presence. He made *The Way* to rescue and legally deliver you and me from Satan who had defrauded us.

God's Law decrees that those who sin will reap the harvest of their sins. *The soul that sins, it shall die.*[Eze.18:4,20] *The wages of sin is death.*[Rom.6:23]

But *all* have sinned.[Rom.3:23; 5:12] *Wherefore, as by one person [Adam] sin entered into the world, and death by sin; so death passed upon all, for all have sinned.*[Rom.5:12] So the harvest of sin was inescapable. All would suffer, degenerate and die.

Only an innocent, sinless One could take our place and assume our judgment on our behalf. If someone without sin would assume and endure all of the punishment that our sins deserved, then we could be exonerated and declared no longer guilty. But since *all* had sinned, no substitute could be found.[Isa.59:16; 63:5]

Then God's Love-idea prevailed. He gave His Son as *a ransom* for us.[1Ti.2:5-6; Mar.10:45] Jesus Christ, the innocent One, suffered the penalty that we deserved, so that we could be acquitted and He could declare us *not guilty.*[Rom.5:9 LB]

That is the message that we declare around the world. It is *The MESSAGE That WORKS.*

CHAPTER THIRTY-ONE

YOUR DEBT IS ABOLISHED

THE GOSPEL IS *Good News*. What Good News? It is the Good News of what Jesus did for us on the Cross. He bore the punishment of our sins so that we do not need to be punished. By expunging our record, He delivered us from the consequences of our sins, which included disease.

The great redemptive chapter of Isaiah 53 says, *Certainly He has borne our sicknesses and carried our pains.*[v.4] When Jesus suffered our penalty on the Cross, *He was being wounded for our transgressions, bruised for our iniquities: the chastisement of our peace was upon Him; and with His stripes we are healed.* Isa.53:5

If Jesus suffered our diseases and bore our pains, then logically *we are healed.*

This is like saying: "Your friend paid your debt, and by his payment, your debt no longer exists. So you are free." Your debt is wiped from the record, once it has been paid. You have no more debt. You cannot pay the same debt twice. Once paid, your debt is expunged.

The *Message* Confirmed

That is God's message of Good News. Jesus said, "When you *know that truth, it makes you free.*" [Joh.8:32] In other words, when that Good News is announced or taught or preached or written or recorded, then heard, it (the Gospel) *is the power of God unto salvation.*[Rom.1:16] It (the Gospel) is the message that Christ *confirms.*[Mar.16:20] He will confirm this truth today, in your life, as you read with faith and reverence.

Jesus announced: *For the Lord has consecrated me and sent me with Good News for people, to heal the brokenhearted, to tell the prisoners **they are free**, to tell captives **they are released**.*[Isa.61:1 (Moffatt)]

Announcing these facts puts God's miraculous power to work among the listeners. This is what we have experienced worldwide. We proclaim these facts. People hear them and believe them, and God manifests them in their lives.

Chapter Thirty-Two

Your Health Is Paid For

THIS MESSAGE OF Good News is, as we stated above, *the power of God for the salvation of everyone who believes it.*^{Rom.1:16}

I cannot explain how Jesus suffered our diseases, bore our pains, and endured the judgment of our sins on the Cross so many years ago, but I believe it. It is not logical. That is why *the preaching of the Cross is to them that perish foolishness: but to us who are saved it is the power of God.*^{1Co.1:18}

When we believe in our hearts and confess with our mouths what the Bible says that Jesus did for us in His vicarious death,^{Rom.10:9-10} then God confirms it by His miracle power. Jesus said, *Only believe.*^{Mar.5:36}

Christ paid for our complete healing when He died. He is the Lord *who heals all our diseases.* [Psa.103:3] He paid for our healing when *He carried our diseases and suffered our pains, taking the stripes by which we were healed.* [Isa.53:4-5 (Literal)]

It is finished now. [Joh.19:30] Our health is paid for. Our diseases were laid upon Christ. [Mat.8:17] He took them away forever. Healing belongs to us now. It is God's gift. This is why the Lord reveals Himself as *the Lord who heals us...the Lord our physician.* [Exo.15:26]

Satan has no right to lay on us what God laid on Jesus Christ at the Cross.

Redemptive Facts For Faith

The Lord has laid on Him the iniquity of us all. [Isa.53:6]

For the transgression of people He was stricken. [v.8]

It pleased the Lord to bruise Him...and make His soul an offering for sin. [v.10]

For He shall bear their iniquity. [v.11]

He bore the sins of many. [v.12]

He was wounded for our transgressions. He was bruised for our iniquities: the chastisement of our peace was upon Him. [v.5]

Certainly He has borne our sicknesses and carried our pains. [v.4 (Literal)] *With His stripes we are healed.* [v.5]

139

Himself took our infirmities, and bare our sicknesses. Mat.8:17 Why? So that we do not have to—so that we can be healed and enjoy health and strength to serve Him by serving people.

He Himself bore our sins in His own body on the tree. Why? *So that we, being dead to sins, should live unto righteousness.* What is the result? *By His stripes we were healed* 1Pe.2:24 —spiritually, mentally, physically.

Deadly Toxins
Life-Giving Gifts

When sin entered the human family, its consequences included physical sickness, malady, suffering and death.

The devastation of deceit and evil, the decadence of lust and envy, the noxious gangrene of hatred and vengeance, the morbid corruption of sin and rebellion all impose their destructive toll on the human body as toxic fall-out.

Salvation and healing are free gifts from God to rescue and to heal human persons, not only from the evil of sin in their hearts and spirits, but from the terrifying physical effects evidenced in the nerves, organs, tissues and glands of their bodies.

This Great Salvation

*Jesus Christ Himself bore **our** sins,*[1Pe.2:24] so that we may be saved and forgiven. *He took **our** infirmities, and bore **our** sicknesses,* [Mat.8:17] so that we may be healed and made whole.

Forgiveness of sins and physical healing are both part of salvation. Spiritual and physical healing, according to God's Word, are to be received together. Salvation includes physical as well as spiritual health. Jesus always healed both.

Total Healing

Who forgives all your iniquities; who heals all your diseases.[Psa.103:3]

Which is it easier to say, Your sins are forgiven you; or to say, Arise, and walk?[Mat.9:5]

*For this people's heart is waxed gross, and their ears dull of hearing, and their eyes they have closed: lest at any time they should see with their eyes, and hear with their ears, and should understand with their heart, and should be **converted**, and I should **heal** them.*[Mat.13:15]

*Is any sick among you?... The prayer of faith shall **save** the sick, and the Lord shall raise them up; and if they have committed sins, they shall be **forgiven**.*[Jam.5:14-15]

The Great Physician offers total health — spiritually, mentally and physically.

141

CHAPTER THIRTY-THREE

CHRIST'S LIFE
IS YOUR LIFE

SINCE JESUS CHRIST bore the sins and diseases of the whole world, He now wants to enter people's lives and become their Savior and their Healer—their Lord.

He said that when we love Him, *the Father will love us, and they would come to us, and make their abode with us.*Joh.14:23

He says, *I am come that you may have life, and that you may have it more abundantly.*Joh.10:10 This new life is for whoever believes.

When you accept Jesus, His abundant and miraculous Life becomes yours. It is not His will that you suffer either sin or disease.

Paul said that *the Life of Jesus might be made manifest (not only in your spirit, but) also in your mortal flesh.*2Co.4:11 Christ's life becomes your life. His righteousness becomes yours. He and the Father *make their abode with you.*Joh.14:23 *You are built for an* **habitation** *of God,*Eph.2:22 *whose* **house** *you are* Heb.3:6 because *Christ* **dwells** *in your heart by faith.* Eph.3:17 *You are the temple of God, and the Spirit of God* **dwells** *in you.*1Co.3:16 *Your* **body** *is the* **temple** *of the Holy Ghost.*1Co.6:19 *Jesus Christ is* **in** *you.*2Co.13:5; Col.1:27 Paul added: *Christ lives* **in** *the believer.*Gal.2:20

The Lord says: *Behold, I stand at the door, and knock: if any one hear my voice, and open the door, I will come in and will sup with them and they with me.* Rev.3:20

Paradise Of Blessings

When humanity's sins were punished and the account of our rebellion was wiped out, anyone who would embrace Christ could then be reconciled to God and restored to the paradise of blessing which He created for people.

Jesus came to the level of our needs and became accountable for our sins. He suffered the punishment we deserved. His blood was shed for us. It washed our record clean.Rev.1:5; Eph.1:7

As soon as any person understands this, the Lord is ready to enter their life. He wants to be their Lord and Savior,(Sect.I) their Peace,(Sect.II) their

Shepherd,(Sect.III) — and their *Physician*.(Sect.IV) He wills that His Life be manifested in you and in me, physically as well as spiritually.

The Bible says, *With long life will I satisfy them and show them my salvation.*Psa.91:10, 16 NRSV

OUR HEALTH IS RENEWED.

Chapter Thirty-Four

The Prayer-Confession

NOW THAT YOU REALIZE where sickness came from and that it was never the design of your Heavenly Father that His children suffer physically, make this confession to Him in humility and in faith.

He invites you: *Call unto me, and I will answer you.*[Jer.33:3] *Ask, and you shall receive, that your joy may be full.*[Joh.16:23-24] *For everyone who asks receives.*[Mat.7:8] Say this to Him aloud:

DEAR LORD: I thank you for announcing that *you are the Lord, my physician.*[Exo.15:26] I am grateful to know that your plan for me includes physical healing.

Before I knew that sickness, suffering and pain resulted from that first rebellion by Adam and Eve, I presumed that there was no escape from physical disease in my life.

Now I know that sickness is part of the result of Adam and Eve being banished from your presence. They were subjugated by Satan whose purpose is *to kill, to steal and to destroy them,*^{Joh.10:10} and disease is part of the consequence of banishment from your divine presence.

You did not abandon us in slavery to the Evil One. After Adam and Eve disobeyed your Word, we all deserved to die. But you sent your Son to be *the propitiation for the sins of the whole world.*^{Rom.3:24-25}

I NOW UNDERSTAND that Jesus suffered not only the punishment of my sins, but also the consequences of my fallen nature, part of which is disease and pain.

Now I know that Jesus Christ *of a certainty took upon Himself all of my diseases and suffered all of my pains* ^{Isa.53:4-5 (Literal)} so that I can be completely *healed.*

Lord, your body was beaten beyond recognition. *Your visage was marred more than any other man.*^{Isa.52:14} Your back was striped. When they beat you, *they plowed your back: they made long their furrows.*^{Psa.129:3} You were bruised and torn.^{Isa.53:5} Now I know that my sicknesses were laid on you.^{Mat.8:17} You suffered them for me so that I could be healed.

146

I THANK YOU LORD, for sending me this message of *Good News*. I receive your miracle life in me, here and now. *By your stripes I have been healed.*Isa.53:5; 1Pe.2:24

The grace and life of Jesus Christ which now abides in me, heals me of both sin and disease. I am saved and healed — and free.

Satan has lost his dominion over me. No sin can subjugate or condemn me. No sickness has the right to destroy my body which is now *the temple of the Holy Spirit.*1Co.6:19

JESUS, YOU ARE MY LORD. From today, I appropriate the blessing of physical healing because you are my Life. You are with me and in me now!Joh.14:17 My *HEALTH IS RENEWED.* Amen!

SECTION IV — HEALTH RENEWED

T.L. and Daisy Osborn have been teammates in evangelism for over half a century, proclaiming the gospel of Christ and sharing His love with millions of people, face to face, in more than 70 nations. Here they rejoice together on the final day of another triumphant soulwinning crusade.

T.L. AND DAISY OSBORN CRUSADES

Over 100 gospel vans, equipped with Evangelism Tools, have been provided for national church organizations worldwide, by the Osborn Ministries, to facilitate them in reaching their nations with the gospel message of Jesus Christ.

OSBORN CRUSADE — Bogota

OSBORN CRUSADE — Accra

OSBORN CRUSADE — Holland

OSBORN CRUS Nigeria

Hundreds of tape-players and thousands of the Osborns'

The Osborns' books and tracts are published in 132 languages, (their docu-miracle crusade films, videos and audio cassettes in 67 languages). These are scattered throughout the world, and are among the most effective Tools for Evangelism known, communicating the gospel to millions of people.

BORN CRUSADE —

OSBORN CRUSADE — Kinshasa

OSBORN CRUSADE — W. Africa

OSBORN CRUSADE Calabar

...assettes, in 67 languages, witness to millions of souls worldwide.

T.L. Osborn ministers the miracle Gospel in Moscow, Russia.

T.L. & LaDonna Osborn Soulwinning and Evangelism Conference

T.L. Osborn ministers under Eckman's 10,000 seat tent, Sweden.

Only miracles can convince the ex-Soviet nations about Christ.

TONS of Osborn books given believers in Antioquia Province, S.Am.

Swedes; famous for Missions, respond to T.L.'s dynamic preaching.

10 Osborn Books in Russian

Top row, left to right: By T.L. 1) The Good Life 2) Soulwinning 3) God's Love Plan 4) The Best of Life 5) Receive Miracle Healing. These are the very best of T.L.'s writings, now in *Russian*, being sown nation-wide.

Bottom row, left to right: By Daisy 1) Woman Without Limits 2) 5 Choices For Women Who Win 3) The Woman Believer 4) New Life For Women 5) Women & Self-Esteem – Dr. Daisy's best, now in *Russian*.

With great care and appreciation, young Russian Gospel ministers unpack T.L. & Daisy's powerful books which have arrived from Belarus, by the Trans-Siberian railway, and have been trucked to the Osborn Miracle-Life Conference at Moscow.

"The Seed is the Word of God"

Thousands of T.L. & Daisy's dynamic books are shipped from the press in Minsk, Belarus, for presentation to believers at each of the ten major Miracle-Life Conferences conducted by T.L. & LaDonna Osborn.

Each book is considered a "Treasure" by the young Russian churches. Jesus said that when the seed falls on "good ground," it will "bring forth." The people of these ex-Soviet republics are fertile soil.

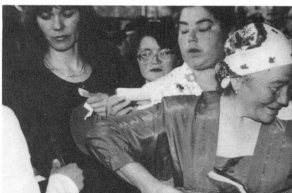

The precious gift of 10 Osborn Books, in Russian, are presented to every preacher, pastor, evangelist, missionary, Bible Teacher, and Gospel worker who has come to the Osborn Miracle-Life Conferences, many traveling vast distances.

T.L. & LaDonna Osborn Crusade - Medellin, Colombia

T.L. & LaDonna Osborn Miracle-Life Conference - Almaty, Kyrghyzstan, an ex-Soviet Republic. The 10 Osborn books in Russian are given to every believer.

T.L. & Daisy Osborn Mass Miracle Crusade - Bogota, S. America

Thousands attend the Osborn Conference in this ancient, Moslem nation of Kyrghyzstan that lies just across the Tien Shan mountain range from west China.

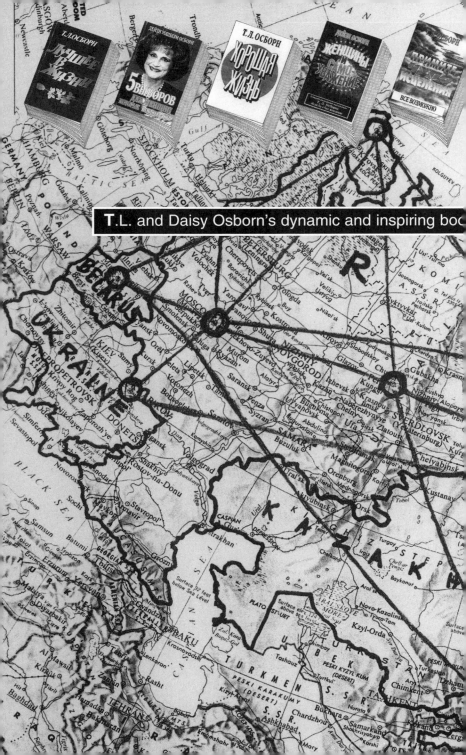

Т.ЛОСБОРН
Лучшее в жизни

ДЭЙЗИ УОШБЕРН ОСБОРН
5 выборов
для женщин,
которые побеждают

Т.Л. ОСБОРН
Хорошая жизнь

ДЭЙЗИ ОСБОРН
Женщина и само-уважение
Т.Л. Осборн and Daisy Osborn

Т.Л ОСБОРН
Динамичная жизнь
Все возможно

T.L. and Daisy Osborn's dynamic and inspiring boo

... *Russian* are now in over <u>400</u> <u>cities</u> <u>and</u> <u>towns.</u>

T.L. & Daisy Osborn Mass Miracle Crusade - Hyderabad, India

T.L. Osborn Teaching Conference, Upsala, Sweden

T.L. Osborn preaching at 50th Anniversary of the Holy Spirit's power in Bangkok, Thailand.

T.L. & Daisy Osborn were the first to bring the miracle ministry to the nation of Thailand in 1956.

The Osborn gospel literature is published in 132 languages. Here Christian workers in Thailand unload a large shipment for soulwinning outreaches there.

The Osborns conduct Evangelism Seminars for Christian workers around the world, like this one in the capitol city of Bangkok, Thailand. (Photos — Top: United in prayer after a strategic teaching session. Bottom: Posing for photograph on the final day of the seminar. Center and opposite page: Equipped for soulwinning outreaches nationwide.

WOMEN'S NATIONAL CONFERENCE — E. AFRICA

Daisy Osborn seeds the women of the world in her national women's mass rallies abroad.

INDONESIAN WOMEN'S DAY — SURABAJA

WOMEN'S NATIONAL MIRACLE DAY — KAMPALA

AUSTRALIAN CONFERENCE

T.L. AND DAISY OSBORN CRUSADES WORLDWIDE. For over half a century, in 73 nations, they have been pace-setters in mass-evangelism. It is believed that they have shared Christ with more non-Christians, face to face, than any couple who has ever lived.

CARIBBEAN — Ponce, Puerto Rico

AFRICA — Kinshas, Zaire

INDONESIA — Surabaya, Java

MEXICO — Monterrey

PHILIPPINES — Cabanatuan

Largest Soulwinning Seminar in Kenya's history, conducted by

Above: Tons of Osborns' Soulwinning Tools for African church leade

rns. 5,000 national church leaders attend from seven nations.

w: The Osborn Soulwinning Seminar, under big Bamboo Cathedral.

T.L. AND DAISY
OSBORN
MASS EVANGELISM
CRUSADES (Cont'd)

WEST AFRICA — Accra, Ghana

MEXICO — Cuidad Juarez

AFRICA — Kampala, Uganda

CARIBBEAN — Ponce, Puerto Rico

TRINIDAD — San Fernando

For almost 54 years, T.L. and Daisy Osborn have shared the miracle Gospel confirmed by signs and wonders with multitudes of people in 73 nations. It is believed that they have preached to more people face to face *in non-Christian nations*, and have won more souls to Christ and witnessed more healing miracles among these multitudes, than any couple in history. Every outreach of their ministries addresses women and men equally, and emphasizes the *Good News that Jesus Christ is the same yesterday, today and forever.* Heb. 13:8

Dr. Daisy proclaims the Gospel at the Municipal Stadium in Surabaya, Java. (Below) Osborn daughter LaDonna, pastor of *Int'l Gospel Center* at Tulsa, OK., preaches Christ at stadium in Papua New Guinea.

T.L. AND DAISY
OSBORN
MASS EVANGELISM
CRUSADES (Cont'd)

HONDURAS — Tegucigalpa

JAPAN — Kyoto

EAST AFRICA — Mombasa, Kenya

PHILIPPINES — Davao, Mindanao

S. AMERICA — Bogota, Colombia

SUPERIMPOSED PHOTOGRAPH

Both T.L. and Daisy Osborn believe and proclaim that "The preaching of the cross ... is the power of God;" that "The Gospel is the power of God unto salvation to every-one that believes." They contend that no one has the right to hear the Good News repeatedly while millions have never hear it at all. Sharing Christ and His love with others is the ministry nearest the heart of God. The life-mission of all believers is to tell others how Jesus came and "gave His life a ransom" to redeem them to God.

Section V

Prosperity Regained

✧ 📖 ✧

GOD - OUR SOURCE
MATERIAL BLESSING

GOD REVEALS HIMSELF BY HIS *REDEMPTIVE* NAME, *JEHOVAH-JIREH,* TRANSLATED *"THE LORD WILL PROVIDE."* GEN.22:8 MATERIAL BLESSINGS ARE *REDEMPTIVE BLESSINGS;* THEY ARE PAID FOR ON OUR BEHALF AND IN OUR NAME WHEN JESUS CHRIST DIED AS OUR SUBSTITUE. BY HIS *GRACE, "THOUGH HE WAS RICH, YET FOR OUR SAKE HE BECAME POOR, THAT WE THROUGH HIS POVERTY MIGHT BE RICH."* 2CO.8:9 SINCE HE DIED FOR US, *"HOW SHALL HE NOT WITH HIM ALSO FREELY GIVE US ALL THINGS?"* ROM.8:32

Chapter Thirty-Five

God's Abundance

WHEN GOD CREATED Adam and Eve, He placed them in a world of material abundance. He commanded the waters and the ground to *bring forth abundantly.*^{Gen.1:20} After creating all living creatures of the land, fowls of the air and fishes of the sea, He *blessed them saying, be fruitful and multiply.*^{Gen.1:22} *And God saw that it was good.*^{Gen.1:25}

Then he placed Adam and Eve in the midst of this garden of bounty, *to dress it and to keep it.*^{Gen.2:15}

But Satan's intervention enticed Adam and Eve to sin against God. Their disobedience resulted in their being separated from His presence, ^{Isa.59:2} exiled from His rich garden of abundance. God said to them: *Cursed is the ground for your sake; in sorrow shall you eat of it all the days of your life; thorns also and thistles shall it bring forth to you;...in the sweat of your face shall you eat bread, until you return to the ground.* Gen.3:17-19

When Rhythm And Harmony Were Lost

That was when material poverty and want became the plight of the human race. Deprivation, destitution, indigence, drought, deficiency and famine have plagued every generation that followed.

The rhythm and harmony of people and of their environment was disrupted, resulting not only in physical disease, but in distrust, loss of integrity, mismanagement and abuse of principles that caused material poverty and destitution.

Humanity has struggled since the fall of Adam and Eve to recover what was forfeited.

Now you can understand the reason for human destitution and material lack — and why God made a way for you to be reconciled to Him so that you can recover the material blessings He originally planned for you.

CHAPTER THIRTY-SIX

THE BEAUTIFUL DESIGN

THE ECONOMIC PROBLEMS which exasperate people are the issue of their deeper problem of estrangement from God

The typical family struggles to meet basic material needs. This is Satan's strategy to break their will and to keep them subjugated.

God never created His children for enslavement and poverty. You and I were not born for material lack and penury.

Material Abundance

The Garden of Eden was a paradise of material abundance. It was the ambiance and lifestyle that

God designed for you and me to live in. It was His dream of contentment, harmony, and blessing for those whom He created *in His own image.*

But then Satan posed his deadly question. Adam and Eve yielded to his temptation to not believe what God had said.^{Gen.3:1} Through their *lust of the flesh and pride of life,*^{1Jo.2:16} they partook of the forbidden fruit which God warned them not to eat, and thereby forfeited the abundance He created for them.^{Gen.3:23-24}

Estranged from God's presence, the seed of sin which had been planted in their spirits began to produce its foreboding harvest ^{Jam.1:14-15} in human lives.^{Rom.1:21-32}

Greed and evil, lust and deceit resulted in a depraved human society where the strong dominated the weak and the rich manipulated the poor. Lords ruled over peasants, males over females.

The venom of resentment, envy, hatred, vengeance and murder continued to smolder in the spirits of the depressed, while a ruthless passion for power and dominance gnawed at their oppressors like a cancer.

Pleasure gave way to anguish. Happiness and love turned to discontentment and lust. Physical health became poisoned by disease. Abundance and material blessing degenerated into want and destitution. God's dream for people had to be suspended until *The Way* of legal reconciliation with Him could be effected.

No Slavery In God's Family

Jesus explained it all when He said: *The thief [Satan] comes only to steal, and to kill, and to destroy.* [Joh.10:10] *But God is not willing that any should perish, but that all should come to repentance.* [2Pe.3:9]

God never intended for any human person, made *in His image and likeness,* to be a slave.

When we were yet without strength, in due time Christ died for the ungodly. [Rom.5:6]

Who is like unto the Lord our God, who dwells on high? He raises up the poor out of the dust, and lifts the needy out of the dunghill. [Psa.113:5-7]

O taste and see that the Lord is good: blessed is the one who trusts in Him. [Psa.34:8] *Christ has delivered you out of the power of darkness.* [Col.1:13] *He delivers and rescues, and He works signs and wonders.* [Dan.6:27; 2Co.1:10; Heb.2:15; 2Ti.4:18]

You and I were born to be *heirs of God — joint-heirs with Jesus Christ.* [Rom.8:16-17; Gal.3:29]

CHAPTER THIRTY-SEVEN

MENTAL CONDITIONING

SINCE ADAM AND EVE yielded to Satan's temptation, his insidious deception has touched every fiber of human life. He has defrauded humanity of everything that is precious until people have become conditioned to poverty and misery. They have succumbed to insolvency.

Most religious teaching implies that God wills indigence and financial scarcity. Church society has been brainwashed to believe that material abundance breeds pride, that spiritual and humble people must live in material poverty, and that physical suffering refines character.

Tap In To The Big Source

But God's redemptive plan provides for abundant blessings of material prosperity, success, happiness and achievement.

What is the secret to enjoying these blessings? How can one tap into this source? If it is not in God's plan for us to live in a state of material need and indigence, what can be done about it?

CHAPTER THIRTY-EIGHT

REBIRTH OF DIVINE WORTH

GOD CREATED THE *heaven and the earth.*^{Gen.1:1}
He created Adam and Eve ^{Gen.1:27} *and breathed into
them his breath of Life and they became living souls.*
Gen.2:7

*By Him all things were created, that are in heaven,
and that are in earth, visible and invisible.*^{Col.1:16}

*It pleased the Father that in Christ should all full-
ness dwell.*^{Col.1:19}

The Holy Scriptures assure us that God, the
Creator and Author of Life, is our limitless and
miraculous source for all that we could ever need
or desire.

God's dream for you and me is that we be full of life, that we enjoy the abundance that He has provided, and that we abound with happiness, health and material blessings.

Sin disrupted God's plan, so that His rich legacy of blessings was forfeited in exchange for a world that would be cursed with disappointment and despair, with depravity and deterioration, with indigence and material insufficiency.

The Price Is Paid

But God's immeasurable love drove Him to make a way for man and woman to regain their lost paradise and, once more, experience the blessings of His abundance, materially as well as spiritually and physically.

Once our sins were punished, there was nothing left to stand between us and God. When we believe the Good News of what Jesus did for us at the Cross, then God welcomes us back to Himself.

Material Blessings Included

Jesus said: *I have come that you may have Life, and have it more abundantly.*[Joh.10:10] The French Bible says that Christ has come *that we might have Life, and be in abundance.*

With sin and rebellion out of the way, we can walk together with God again. He wills no poverty, scarcity, lack or penury. His redemptive plan guarantees abundant material blessings.

Jesus Christ came *to destroy the works of the devil,* [1Jo.3:8] which include sin and every evil consequence that weakens and demoralizes humanity, including material poverty.

Merchandising For Filthy Lucre's Sake

I am including a litany of Bible promises and statements about God's material blessings for your encouragement and faith.

Much abuse has been made of certain verses by people who, *with feigned words make merchandise of the public,* [2Pe.2:3] *teaching things...for filthy lucre's sake.* [Tit.1:10-11]

Because of the proliferation of contemporary "prosperity" pontificates through public media, I must remind the reader that Bible teaching about prosperity never encourages *heaping up riches* [Psa.39:6] or *laying up treasure for one's self without being rich toward God.* [Luk.12:21]

Material Prosperity
Without God's Perspective

Before listing Bible statements that encourage material blessing, one must observe that the negative influence of material riches is also biblical when not linked to witnessing for Christ among the *un*-converted.

Jesus spoke of *the deceitfulness of riches,*Mat.13:22 and Paul said *the love of money is the root of all evil* — not money itself, but the *love* of it — then added, *which while some coveted after, have erred from the faith, and pierced themselves through with many sorrows.*1Ti.6:10

Another alert from Jesus concerned how *the cares of this world, the deceitfulness of riches, and the lusts of things can choke the Word so that it becomes unfruitful* in one's life.Mar.4:19

One day the Lord *looked around, and said to His disciples, How hard it is for those who have riches and...for those who* **trust** *in riches...to enter the kingdom of God!*Mar.10:23-24

Jesus warned, *Woe unto you that are rich! for you have received your consolation.*Luk.6:24 That can happen if one seeks material blessing for prosperity's sake, *laying up treasure for one's self, and not being rich toward God.*Luk.12:21

The Apostle Paul reminded Timothy and the believers at Ephesus, *They that will be rich fall into*

191

temptation and a snare, and into many foolish and hurtful lusts, which drown people in destruction and perdition. Charge them that are rich in this world, that they be not highminded, nor **trust** *in uncertain riches, but in the living God, who gives us richly all things to enjoy.*[1Ti.6:9-17]

Traditional Teaching
A *Prosperity-Phobia*

Traditional Christian teaching has so emphasized these warnings about material prosperity that believers have associated poverty with spirituality and material wealth with ungodliness. This creates a *prosperity phobia* which has impeded the promulgation of the Gospel.

Christian believers are members of God's Royal Family. We are commissioned and trusted by our Lord [1Ti.1:11; 1Th.2:4] to give the Gospel to *every creature in all the world.*[Mar.16:15] That requires money. That is why God wills that His children prosper materially in the same way that their souls prosper spiritually.[3Jo.2]

Abundant Promises

With a balanced and biblical perspective of material blessings, these statements that follow can nourish your faith and courage to expect His material blessings to prosper you as a believer whose heart is set on propagating the Good News to the *un*-converted.

O *fear the Lord, you His saints: for there is no want to them that fear Him.*[Psa.34:9]

They that seek the Lord shall not want any good thing.[Psa.34:10]

My God shall supply all your need.[Phi.4:19]

I wish above all things that you may prosper.[3Jo.2] (This word, *prosper*, implies general prosperity in life, including, but not limited to, material prosperity.)

For the Lord...has pleasure in the prosperity of His servants.[Psa.35:27]

The Lord will make you plenteous in goods, in the fruit of your body, and in the fruit of your cattle, and in the fruit of your ground.[Deu.28:11]

The Lord will open to you His good treasure.[Deu.28:12]

The blessing of the Lord brings wealth.[Pro.10:22 NIV]

The Lord shall command the blessing upon you...in all that you set your hand to.[Deu.28:8]

The Only Condition

The condition is to *only believe* [Mar.5:36; Heb.11:6] the Gospel message that Christ redeemed you from your sins and from their effects,[Gal.3:13] part of which is material poverty.

That is salvation. That is deliverance from the power and influence of Satan over our lives. That is freedom from the death sentence of sin, from the plague of disease, from material lack, and from all the *works of the devil*.[1Jo.3:8]

That is what we have taught multitudes for over half a century, worldwide. That is what Christ confirms.[Mar.16:20] That is *The MESSAGE That WORKS*.

Chapter Thirty-Nine

God's Material Blessings

NOW YOU CAN experience *Life* in fellowship and friendship with God and experience His material blessings for carrying out His plan.

When you understand His ideal for your life, you experience a rebirth of self-worth. You realize that He wills for you to enjoy material as well as spiritual and physical blessings.

Bible Verses That Build Faith

Here are more verses from the Bible for your encouragement:

Honor the Lord with your substance, and with the firstfruits of all your increase: so shall your barns be filled with plenty.[Pro.3:9-10]

He challenges you to *bring of your money to Him [your tithes], and prove Him with it now...and see if He will not open you the windows of heaven, and pour you out a blessing, that there shall not be room enough to receive.*[Mal.3:10]

For the Lord God says...*the barrel of meal shall not waste, neither shall the cruse of oil fail.*[1Ki.17:14]

For the earth is the Lord's and the fullness thereof.
[1Co.10:26]

Riches and wealth are the gift of God.[Ecc.5:19]

You shall make your way prosperous, and you shall have good success.[Jos.1:8]

Seek first the expansion of God's Kingdom worldwide, and all these things shall be added unto you.
[Mat.6:33 RV]

The Lord is your Shepherd, you shall not want.
[Psa.23:1]

No good thing will He withhold from them that walk uprightly.[Psa.84:11]

Blessed is anyone who fears the Lord, who delights greatly in His commandments...wealth and riches shall be in his or her house.[Psa.112:1, 3]

You shall remember the Lord your God: for it is He who gives you power to get wealth.[Deu.8:18]

The silver is mine, and the gold is mine.^{Hag.2:8} *All the earth is mine.*^{Exo.19:5} *The land is mine.*^{Lev.25:23} *Every beast of the forest is mine, and the cattle on a thousand hills.*^{Psa.50:10} *How excellent is Your loving kindness, O God! Therefore...people put their trust under...Your wings. They shall be abundantly satisfied...for with You is the fountain (source) of Life.*^{Psa.36:7-9}

The blessing of the Lord makes rich, and He adds no sorrow with it.^{Pro.10:22}

O Lord, how manifold are Your works.... the earth is full of Your riches;... You open Your hands, they are filled with good.^{Psa.104:24, 28}

Those who seek me early shall find me. Riches and honor are with me; yes, durable riches and righteousness...that I may cause those who love me to inherit substance; and I will fill their treasures.^{Pro.8:17-18, 21}

Blessed are You, Lord God,...for all that is in the heaven and in the earth is Yours...both riches and honor come from You.^{1Ch.29:10-12}

Walk in God's ways...that you may prosper in all that you do and wherever you turn yourself.^{1Ki.2:3}

Blessed is the Lord, who daily loads us with benefits.
Psa.68:19

A faithful person shall abound with blessings.
Pro.28:20; Deu.29:9

I am come that you may have Life, and that you may have it more abundantly.^{Joh.10:10}

The Abounding Evidence

The world of material wealth that God has created around you is proof that He wills material as well as spiritual and physical blessings for His children.

There is no one who has left house, or brothers, or sisters, or father, or mother, or wife, or children, or lands, for my sake, and the Gospel's, but she or he shall receive a hundredfold now in this time, houses and loved ones and lands,...and in the world to come eternal Life.[Mar.10:29-30]

CHAPTER FORTY

GOD'S BEST FOR YOU

SINCE OUR SINS were put away by Christ, He offers us His Life. By a miracle of His grace, we have been redeemed out of the jurisdiction of Satan and we are now restored to the family of God who says, *I will receive you, and will be a Father to you, and you shall be my sons and daughters.*2Co.6:17-18

Jesus said: *If you then...know how to give good gifts to your children, how much more shall your Father who is in heaven give good things to them who ask Him.*Mat.7:11

*No good thing will He withhold from them who walk uprightly.*Psa.84:11

The Bible says: *Like a parent pities [Hebrew meaning, "loves or shows compassion for"] its children, so the Lord pities them who fear Him.*[Psa.103:13]

God's Family Blessings

Can you imagine a parent who does not desire material blessings for his or her children? Or what parents would desire that their children live in poverty and destitution?

God, your heavenly Father, desires that you enjoy His best in this life, materially as well as physically and spiritually.

Poverty And Sickness
Eulogized As Blessings

If people had not been brain-washed to believe that prosperity produces pride and that poverty fosters humility, then this information would make good sense. God is good and rich and abundant. He created all of earth's riches. He loves His children. And He desires that they be blessed materially.

But poverty is like sickness. Tradition has erroneously eulogized both of these plagues as instruments of God's mysterious blessing which, many say, will produce humility, patience, submission and obedience to Him.

Many people have made a religion of both their suffering and their poverty. I learned long ago that people will fight to defend their religion, so I know to be careful about what I say or write about these two issues.

I also learned that if people relate their poverty to piety in any way, then before they can experience God's material blessings, they need a new perspective of material wealth.

From God's big viewpoint, the riches He created and placed on our planet [Gen.2:9-14] are not for the unbelieving world to monopolize, but they are created to facilitate His people who carry out His commission as Christ's witnesses in this world.

I've included this section in this book to project God's attitude about His material provisions, so that Christian believers will have faith 1) to appropriate the wealth God has placed here, 2) to enjoy the lifestyle that He wills for His children, and 3) to use His material wealth to fulfill His plan for humanity.

Chapter Forty-One

Faith For Abundance

HERE IS A PREVAILING Bible principle: To receive any blessing that Christ died to provide, you must believe that He wills that you receive it. We call this *faith*.

All of His blessings come to us through faith. *Without faith it is impossible to please Him: for whoever comes to God must believe that He is, and that He is a rewarder of them that diligently seek Him.*[Heb.11:6]

That is why Jesus said, *Only believe,*[Mar.5:36] and *Whatever you desire, when you pray, believe that you receive it, and you shall have it.*[Mar.11:24]

Our Part Is To *Only Believe*

Even though Christ died to open *The Way* to His blessings, in order to receive them we must believe His Word. To do that, we must be convinced that the blessings that Christ died to provide are available to all persons for whom He died. There are no exceptions. Redemption is for all.

Convinced that Jesus Christ died on our behalf, we express that faith by receiving Him, by confessing Him publicly,[Rom.10:9-10] and by expecting to receive the blessings He died to provide.

The Fatal Suggestion

Satan, who continues to be our insidious enemy, seeks to defraud us and to influence us to question God's promises. He maneuvers situations, distorting facts and plotting negative thoughts, to suggest that God does not mean what he says in His Word.

To discredit the validity of God's promise is Satan's subtle strategy. That is sin—the original sin that separated Adam and Eve from God's presence and blessings. Satan has no new strategy, no new deception. He simply lures new people into his age-old traps of unbelief by suggesting that God's Word is not to be taken seriously.

Satan is a liar.[Joh.8:44] He despises and disparages faith in God. He is like a dishonest lawyer who defrauds people of their legal inheritance.

Faith – Not Frustration

Satan will steal all of God's redemptive blessings from you if he can. He does it; by lying to you, tricking you, confusing you with negative suggestions or traditional teachings; by causing you to look at symptoms more than at God's Word; by instilling fear that you might become proud or arrogant if you are blessed; and by other deceptive lies contrived to *steal and to kill and to destroy* you and the blessings that God wills for you to enjoy.[Joh.10:10]

That is why Paul encouraged us to *fight the good fight of faith.*[1Ti.6:12] In other words, we are to stand up and believe God's Word. We are to claim and possess the blessings He has provided, even when suggestions discredit them and when evidence makes them look or seem incredible.

We walk by faith, not by sight.[2Co.5:7]

In Christ's redemptive death, He took our sins and bore all of their consequences. He wills that we live in the abundance of His blessings.

That is His plan for YOU. That is the Good News that Christ confirms by miracles, signs and wonders. That is *The MESSAGE That WORKS.*

Chapter Forty-Two

Adopting
A New Life

To COMPREHEND THE intimate partnership and friendship that God wills for you is of supreme importance in your life. Since He is *Love*, understand that the principle of Love is to GIVE. *God so loved that He **gave**.*[Joh.3:16]

Giving is planting. The law of *seedtime and harvest* [Gen.8:22] guarantees two things: 1) *When we sow, then we shall reap a harvest of the same species that we sowed.*[Gal.6:7] 2) *And we shall reap from what we sowed, in multiplied form.*[2Co.9:6]

The seeds of God's Life are planted in us as we embrace His Good News. Then we become planters of those seeds in the lives of others to produce His blessings in them too.

Planting Always Brings Harvest

We plant kindness, then more of it comes back to us. We plant service and help, then we reap a harvest of the same. We plant praise and encouragement, then those virtues flow back to us in multiplied form. We plant money in God's work, then He returns to us a harvest of material blessings. That is His law of sowing and reaping. It cannot fail.

We plant in faith the same as a farmer who sows seed in faith that a harvest will result. Then in prayer we claim God's abundant return and His law of sowing and reaping brings it to pass.

We refuse to give credit to contradictory evidence. We do not listen to negative reasoning. We resist the snare of pious tradition that glorifies poverty as producing humility. We rebuff, in prayer and faith, any attempt by Satan to prevent us from receiving material, as well as spiritual or physical blessings. [3Jo.2]

We adopt God's new Love-Life. We discover the blessing of giving, because what we give is what we plant and what we plant is what produces our harvest.

The Abundant Return

We learn why the Lord Jesus said *it is more blessed [productive] to give than to receive.*[Acs.20:35]

Jesus said, *Give, and it shall be given unto you; good measure, pressed down, and shaken together, shall people give into your bosom.*[Luk.6:38]

Solomon said: *Honor the Lord with your substance, and with the firstfruits (not leftovers) of all your increase: so shall your barns be filled with plenty.*[Pro.3:9-10]

You shall eat in plenty and be satisfied, and praise the name of the Lord.[Joe.2:26]

Money For God's Purpose

Christians see money and material plenty not only as blessings for their personal lives, but more importantly, as provisions for the Lord's work. That is why God has provided the wealth of this planet, and it is why He wills that His children utilize it for both their own blessing and for the blessing of sharing His love with others.

Certainly when people *love silver, they shall never be satisfied.*[Ecc.5:10] But the Christian believer learns that God's plan of material blessing is for the sake of carrying out His plan for people.

The rich fool who ignored God and *stored up his goods for himself* was condemned,[Luk.12:19-20] and so is any person who *lays up treasure for himself or herself.*[Luk.12:21]

Learning to plant, then to harvest more, is learning to be a partner with God, serving Him

by serving people, giving the *Gospel to every creature.* Mar.16:15

That is what we have taught millions, and I can
tell you, it is *The MESSAGE that WORKS.* God's
power is behind His Word to make it good for
whoever believes.

The blessing of PROSPERITY IS REGAINED.

CHAPTER FORTY-THREE

THE PRAYER-CONFESSION

THE ONLY REASON we can inherit God's material blessings and the only reason we can be certain that *He shall supply all our needs* Phi.4:19 is that Jesus Christ redeemed us from sin and its consequences (part of which is material poverty).

Since God created a world of abundance for His children, it is His will that we enjoy it.

So bring your material and financial needs to the Lord who promises to *supply all your need.* Phi.4:19 He will do it even if He must perform a material miracle like feeding the multitude Mat.14; Mar.6; Luk.9; Joh.6 or turning water into wine Joh.2:3-10 or causing the cruse of oil to flow 2K.4:3-6 or the meal not to cease. 1K.17:14-16 His miraculous power is not limited to spiritual wonders. He performs physical and material miracles too.

Make this confession to Him, aloud:

DEAR LORD: I thank you for your promises of material abundance for my life. You do not will poverty and need, any more than you will sin and sickness.

I am thankful to know that your *great salvation* [Heb.2:3] delivers me not only from my sins, but from their consequences—from *all the works of the devil* [1Jo.3:8] that have been sent *to steal, kill and destroy* my heritage. [Joh.10:10]

When you created material abundance in this earth, you demonstrated that you want your children to enjoy it and to utilize it.

You placed rich treasures here, [Gen.2:9-14] not for *un*-believers to monopolize, but for the prosperity, facility and blessing of your children who carry out your will among people.

THANK YOU, LORD. Your Word says, I *shall not lack any good thing.* [Psa.34:10] *You shall supply all of my need.* [Phi.4:19] *You wish, above all things, that I prosper and be in health, even as my soul prospers.* [3Jo.2]

THANK YOU, LORD, that *you have pleasure in the prosperity of your servants.* [Psa.35:27] Thank you for your promise *to make me plenteous in goods.* [Deu.28:11] I believe that you have *commanded your blessing upon me... in all that I set my hand to.* [Deu.28:8]

THE PRAYER-CONFESSION

I believe that *Christ redeemed me from the curse* Gal.3:13 of poverty and evil, of lack and destitution.

I WILL, FROM THIS DAY, *honor you with my substance and with the firstfruits (not leftovers) of all my increase: So shall my barns be filled with plenty.*Pro.3:9-10

I now know that *the earth is the Lord's and the fullness thereof.*1Co.10:26 I realize now that *riches and wealth are the gift of God.*Ecc.5:19 So long as I do not *love money* 1Ti.6:10 or seek to store it up or trust in riches,Mar.10:24; 1Ti.6:17 *you will make my way prosperous, and I shall have good success.*Jos.1:8

I will bring my firstfruits (my first and my best), my *tithes* and my *offerings* to you for your work, as you commanded,Mal.3:10 and I shall *prove* your Word by acting upon it. I believe you will *open heaven's windows and pour me out blessings* and harvests of much more than I bring to you, according to your promise. Mal.3:10

I understand that loving is giving, and giving is planting, and *whatever I sow, I shall also reap—more.*Gal.6:7

I WILL BEGIN planting. And since you are the God of miracles, I know that even if it requires a material miracle, like multiplying the boy's lunch to feed a multitude,Mat.14: Mar.6: Luk.9: Joh.6: you will do it to guarantee my harvest. Your Word *cannot return to you void* Isa.55:11 and *the Scriptures cannot be broken.*Joh.10:35

211

I now realize that, although there is suffering and poverty around me, this is Satan's work — not yours. You do not will these evils anymore than you will that we live in sin.

I AM YOUR CHILD. You are my Father. I have my roots in *Divine Royalty.*2Co.6:16; 1Pe.2:9

You were rich, yet for my sake you became poor, that I through your poverty might be rich 2Co.8:9 ...materially as well as physically and spiritually.

You are my Creator and you live in me. I am a blessed member of your Royal Family where *PROSPERITY IS REGAINED*. Amen!

Section VI

Friendship Resumed

✧ 📖 ✧

FRIENDSHIP COMPANIONSHIP
AT ONE WITH GOD

GOD REVEALS HIMSELF BY HIS *REDEMPTIVE* NAME, *JEHOVAH-SHAMMAH,* TRANSLATED *"THE LORD IS THERE"* OR *"THE LORD IS PRESENT."* EZE.48:35 FRIENDSHIP WITH GOD IS A REDEMPTIVE BLESSING, PAID FOR ON YOUR BEHALF AND IN OUR NAME BECAUSE *"WE WERE MADE NIGH BY THE BLOOD OF CHRIST"* EPH.2:13 WHO PROMISED, *"I WILL NEVER LEAVE YOU, NOR FORSAKE YOU."* HEB.13:5

CHAPTER FORTY-FOUR

KNOW YOUR IDENTITY

THE UNIVERSAL need among human persons is to be acquainted with God, to have fellowship with Him, to share His Life and love, to know that He is present in their lives, and to be at peace with Him.

Whether you have thought about it or not, this craving is in everyone. It is born in you because you are the offspring of God, *created in His image and likeness.*Gen.1:26-27; 5:1-2

It is as normal for people to share Life with God as it is for fish to swim in water or for birds to fly in the sky.

You are a God-person. You are His kind of being. God's breath of divine Life which is in you makes you *a living soul*,[Gen.2:7] created *in His image*.

Our Natural Habitat

You were created to be a partner and friend with God in His Garden of Abundance. That is your natural habitat. You are created to walk with Him. Without God, your potential in life can never be realized.

Each year tens of thousands of people take their own lives, rather than continue in their confused jungle without God.

Each year millions of dollars are spent on fortune tellers. Frantic seekers pay misguided people to give them answers that do not solve problems, and comfort that does not assuage confusion.

Despite the flood of contemporary entertainment, boredom plagues human society.

But why are people apathetic, lonely and empty? It is because they do not know God who created them to be His friends and partners. They can never know fulfillment apart from personal friendship with Him.

You were designed to walk with God.

Gods That Do Not Satisfy

People who do not know God inevitably create gods after their own imaginations. When the living God is not at the center of life, then people look for other gods to usurp His place. Some may even become gods unto themselves.

Rather than honor the Creator, people seek their own way, then become bored with the way they seek. They do as they please but are not pleased with their doing.

Discover your roots your Creator, and respond to His plan of redemption. Then you can inherit the abundant benefits of His Love and Life.

Chapter Forty-Five

The Search
The Discovery

WITHOUT GOD, people are lonely. They need someone they can love and trust. They search for purpose and meaning in life. They need someone to believe in and someone who believes in them—someone they can share with, who will not betray or accuse or judge them. They need to be loved and trusted. They are the offspring of God who *is Love.*[1Jo.4:8,16]

Companionship is basic to human need. When people develop no rapport with other people, they often engage in one-sided conversations with animals, or surroundings, or with themselves or even with plant life.

Grasping Cheap Substitutes

To satisfy this fundamental craving for friend-ship with God, innumerable forms of religion have been conceived: communion with spirits, worship of the sun, moon and stars, trees, flying creatures, animals, insects—even precious stones and carved or sculpted forms.[Rom.1:21-23]

All of this depicts humanity's innate search to rediscover God their Creator. As a suckling child yearns for the solace of its mother's bosom, so every person senses a yearning for God.

One's search may express itself in philosophy or education, amusement or some kind of relig-ion. It all represents a pathetic quest for identity, for purpose, for destiny.

Emptiness Expressed In Body Language

Without God and His companionship, people betray their loneliness by the look in their eyes and by the way they walk. Their body language broadcasts their need. Their vain use of leisure time announces their aimlessness. Their quest for pleasure reveals their emptiness.

Something gnaws inside all human beings who have not identified with God through His plan of salvation. Life for them becomes a bewildering dilemma and a vexing enigma.

Youth may express this longing by destructive rages, promiscuity, demonstrations, escapades and riots. People may become vengeful and reactionary, violent toward their government, instructor, employer, family—or even toward themselves.

Bankruptcy, incurable physical diseases, emotional cop-outs and suicide can be symptoms of one's unfulfilled search for rapport with God.

The Offer Of A New Beginning

There is Good News. Somebody loves you very much. *Greater love has no one than this, that you lay down your life for your friends.*Joh.15:13

That is what Jesus did for YOU. *God so loved you that He gave His best for you. He gave His only begotten Son.*Joh.3:16 He wants to become your lifelong companion and partner from this very day. He wants to be present in your life, and He promises to *never leave you nor forsake you.*Heb.13:5

Chapter Forty-Six

God's Open Door

AROUND THE WORLD in nearly eighty nations, my wife and I have dealt with people of all ages and all classes of society from jungle villagers to university graduates, from privates to generals, from beggars to heads of state, from teenagers to octogenarians.

We have ministered to multitudes of people representing almost every major religion in our world and we have observed that they are searching and probing for deeper meaning in life.

Their perpetual quest is never gratified until they discover that God created them in His own likeness so that they can share His Life with Him.

Although this lofty privilege was forfeited by Adam and Eve, Jesus Christ opened *The Way* for every human person to be redeemed to God and to be miraculously restored to live in His presence with peace and happiness.

Paralyzing Pessimism

This generation has more knowledge and more facilities to assimilate that knowledge than any other in history. But because the idea of God is often disdained, the more that people learn, the more they seem to be adrift without a rudder. Neuroses, hypertension, fear and paralyzing pessimism dominate much of human existence.

Without God, there are no answers to the basic questions of life. As long as people exclude God from their knowledge, despair, confusion and insecurity dominate society.

The world's modern technology, mechanical automation, luxurious living, high-powered automobiles, color television, plus satellite and laser-beam communications can never satisfy the inner longings of humanity for God.

Only when people are restored to their Creator, as His friends and companions, drawing their substance from Him, their true Source, can they be satisfied and rediscover true fulfillment.

Rapport With God

When you dwell in the secret place of the most High, you shall abide under the shadow of the Almighty. Say of the Lord, He is my fortress; in Him will I trust. He shall deliver me. He shall cover me. I shall not be afraid. No evil shall befall me. He shall give His angels charge over me. He will deliver me. With long life will He satisfy me and show me His salvation.[Psa.91]

You will show me the path of Life: in Your presence is fullness of joy; at Your right hand there are pleasures for ever more.[Psa.16:11]

When you discover your roots in God and embrace true friendship with Him, you realize fullness of joy.

Companionship
Friends And Partners

Loneliness and isolation are not God's design for human life. To be misunderstood and unloved is not God's plan. To live without companionship and friends is foreign to God's plan for people. To feel cast aside, excluded, ostracized and without purpose is demoralizing and destructive.

God has a glorious plan for our lives. He desires our company. He wants to share His Life with us as our Greatest Friend and Partner.

He loves us and longs for our friendship so much that He gave His Son to die for our sins so that every wall of separation between us and Him could be removed.[Joh.3:15; Eph.2:13-14, 16]

Now He says: *Behold, I stand at the door and knock: if you hear my voice, and open the door, I will come in to you, and will sup with you, and you with me.*[Rev.3:20]

Fellowship is drinking from the same cup, sharing the same life. The Gospel is the glorious record of how God opened the door for you and me to come back into His presence, and of how He sent His Son to make this possible.

He promises: *Lo, I am with you alway.*[Mat.28:20] His will is to be present in our lives

CHAPTER FORTY-SEVEN

YOU CAN TRUST ME
I WILL TRUST YOU

WHEN GOD FIRST created Adam and Eve, they lived in His presence and enjoyed daily rapport with Him. They had no consciousness of sin or guilt or fear or inferiority. They were like children with loving parents.

Their rightful place was at God's side, sharing life and daily friendship with Him. They lived in close relationship. Their lifestyle was a garden of blessings.

Royalty Never Cowers

God never planned for His children to cower in shame, nor be abandoned in loneliness, nor be excluded from His company. He never planned that they would plead, like indigents, for His favors, trying to impress Him with sacrifices or miserable acts of penitence.

God and Adam and Eve were friends. He created them to be one with Him in populating and developing this planet. The couple God created was involved in His purpose. That is His will for you and me today.

Adam and Eve were never created to be robots. They could choose His friendship and fellowship — and we can too. Or, if they did not want to share Life with Him, then their right of choice would still be honored — and ours will be too.

The Right Of Choice

God never forced Adam and Eve to love Him or to share Life with Him. He has proven that He desires our comradeship but He never obliges or constrains it. You and I have the right of choice.

He warned Adam and Eve that if they ate of the *tree of the knowledge of good and evil, in the day that they ate it, they would surely die.*[Gen.2:16-17] Then He left them with their freedom of choice.

Unfortunately, they both yielded to the influence of Satan who suggested that God did not mean what He had said and added his outright lie: *You shall **not** surely die.*[Gen.3:4] Adam and Eve believed Satan's lie and questioned God's Word.

That was the original sin and it is still the ultimate sin that separates people from God — not to trust what He says.

The *"Deal"* Was Simple

God's rapport and fellowship with His children from the beginning was simple. In essence, He said, "You can always trust Me! I will always trust you!" That is still the basis of His companionship with us. (Get my book *God's Love Plan*.)

When Adam and Eve listened to Satan's lie and did what the Lord God forbade them to do, they were banished from His presence. An angel was placed at the gate of the Garden of Eden with a flaming sword to prevent any possibility of their re-entry into God's presence.Gen.3:24

Now we shall see what God did to impress upon humankind that His presence cannot be violated by sin and that He cannot cohabit with unrighteousness.

Chapter Forty-Eight

The Way Home

FOR THOUSANDS OF YEARS, until the flood came upon the earth, no one could return to the Holy Presence of God in the Garden of Eden.

The abundant Life that flourished there was no longer accessible. Outside the garden, the earth was cursed under the feet of those precious people whom God had created in His own image.

He said, *Cursed is the ground for your sake; in toil you shall eat of it all the days of your life. Both thorns and thistles it shall bring forth to you; and you shall eat the herb of the field.* Gen.3:17-18

Stories About Eden

Oftentimes I ponder the enchanting stories that must have been passed from one generation to another about the lush abundance and beauty of that Garden of Eden where foreparents Adam and Eve once lived, walked and talked with God.

The consequences of sin beleaguered people's lives and plagued their journey. These poisonous evils infected them biologically, erupting in all kinds of disease, suffering and pain. Death and destruction swept over them like tidal waves, devastating the fruits of their labors and obliterating their fondest dreams.

They had cast their lot with Satan. Now they were reaping the consequences of their choice. And that has never changed.

The generations that followed Adam and Eve could not know God in the way that He had been known before. People longed for His presence. They searched for ways to appease Him. But their choice had been to violate His laws. *The penalty for their sins was death.*[Eze.18:4,20]

Illustrating Redemption

Generations later, God called a man named Abraham and made a blood covenant with him. That agreement would be an illustration of His plan for the redemption of humankind.

He gave His Law with its system of priesthood and sacrifices to Abraham's descendants.

This blood covenant embraced the idea of temporarily atoning for (or covering) the sins of people by slaying an innocent animal as a substitute for the one who had sinned.

The writer of Hebrews said later, *It was not possible that the blood of bulls and of goats should take away sins.*[Heb.10:4] It served only as a temporary covering that indicated temporary pardon for people from their sins.

The Complex Interim System

God formalized this complex, interim system of offering animals as substitutes for people, to teach respect for His laws and to impress upon them the sanctity of His presence. It also provided a way for them to approach God—even though at a distance and only through the mediation of a priest who functioned with a sense of utter depravity, fear, guilt and inferiority.

That ceremony, or covenant, afforded a formal way to satisfy, temporarily, humanity's innate passion for relationship with God. That yearning is still in evidence today, portrayed by the religious and superstitious practices of millions who have not heard or believed the Gospel.

Everything about those Old Testament rituals of priesthood and the formalities of animal sacrifices was to accentuate the awesome holiness and righteousness of God's presence which Adam and Eve had flagrantly violated by disregarding the integrity of His Word.

The ceremonial rituals of the Old Covenant Law constituted a *schoolmaster* [Gal.3:23-25] to impress on humankind, not only the holiness of God's presence, but also—and equally vital—the impossibility of sin co-existing with Him. This was the first stage of recovery in the redemption of humanity.

God Amidst The People

Later, Moses who descended from Abraham, was given instructions to *build a tabernacle* [Exo.25:8-9; Acs.7:44] where God could dwell within the encampment of His people—as near to them as His righteousness could permit—and where they could approach Him in ceremonial protocol with scrupulous priestly mediation.

Inside that great tent, or *tabernacle* as it was called, [Exo.33:7] Moses was directed to construct an enclosure to be known as the *Most Holy Place*, and God's presence was to be there. He promised to meet the people and to speak to them there. [Exo.29:42, 45-46; Heb.9:3] He wants to be with people.

No individual could come into that most holy sanctuary where God's sacred presence dwelled, except a certain priest—and he, only once a year. [Exo.30:10; Heb.9:7-8]

The Priest With Bells

The priest had to be covered by a cloud of incense as he entered carrying a basin with the blood of an animal that had been slain. He sprinkled that blood upon the altar in the Holy Chamber to give evidence that an innocent animal had been slain as a substitute for his own sins and for the sins of the people he represented.

Bells were sewn to the priest's garment because, if he had committed iniquity, he would die inside the Holy Chamber.[Exo.28:34-35,43] The ceasing of the bells would alert the people to what had happened. [The priest's] *sound shall be heard when he goes into the holy place before the Lord, and when he comes out, that he die not.*[v.35]

God was teaching them—and us—that what had happened in the Garden of Eden must never be repeated, and that they must comprehend the absolute sanctity of His presence and the total integrity of His Word.

CHAPTER FORTY-NINE

NEVER ALONE AGAIN

WHILE THE OLD Testament Law and its priestly rituals served as a *schoolmaster,*[Gal.3:24-25] it did not satisfy the heart of God. As generations passed, the priesthood degenerated into a lucrative enterprise. Priests heaped to themselves personal gain by profaning the offerings of the people[1Sa.2:13-17] and by seizing for themselves part of the sacrifices which they could later market.

Degeneration And Apostasy

They trafficked in animals and fowls to be offered upon the altar. Some of them even lay with the women who came to the temple to offer sacrifices.[1Sa.2:17,22]

Callused by their apostasy,[Isa.56:11] they made such a mockery of their sacrifices that God expressed in abhorrence: *To what purpose is the multitude of your sacrifices to me? I am full of burnt offerings...I delight not in the blood of bullocks, or of lambs, or of he goats...Bring no more vain oblations; incense is an abomination unto me...Wash you, make you clean...Though your sins be as scarlet, they shall be as white as snow.*[Isa.1:11-18]

God Could Wait No Longer

In the fullness of time,[Gal.4:4] God could wait no longer, and He began His final plan to bring us back into *His holy presence.* He came to our world in the form of a baby to reveal *Himself in the flesh,*[Joh.1:14] and to illustrate, in a human body, the life that He planned for us to be able to live.

Jesus Christ was conceived of the Holy Ghost,[Mat.1:20; Luk.1:35] and was born of a *virgin.*[Mat.1:23; Luk.1:27] Since the bloodline descends from the seed of the father rather than from the mother, and since the seed planted in the womb of the Virgin Mary was created by a miracle,[Luk.1:34-35] the blood of Jesus Christ was divine, not human.[Lev.17:11]

That is why *His blood could be shed for the remission of our sins.*[Mat.26:28] That is why He is *the Lamb of God, who takes away the sin of the world.*[Joh.1:29] That is why *His soul was made an offering for sins.*[Isa.53:10] That is why *Christ put away sin by the sacrifice of*

Himself.[Heb.9:26] That is why *He redeemed us to God by His blood.*[Rev.5:9]

Jesus Showed Us God

As Jesus grew to adulthood, He shocked everyone, especially the religious leaders, by talking about God and with God as intimately as a child relates to its parents.

When He spoke of God as His Father, the people of his epoch considered his words to be blasphemy and sacrilege.[Joh.5:18] He was the first person to call God *His Father.*

They tried to stone Him.[Joh.10:29-33] They plotted to assassinate Him. Finally, through mob-violence, they obtained authority to have Him crucified. [Mat.27:24-26] They screamed, *He makes God His Father; this is blasphemy, and He must die for it!*[Mat.26:65-67; Joh.19:6-7, 15-16]

This fulfilled the prophecies about Christ. [Mat.26:56; 27:35] Religion had so blinded the people and their leaders that they failed to perceive what God was accomplishing. Had they not been obsessed with their own bigotry, they would have recognized that Christ's arrest, accusation and crucifixion had all been foretold by their own prophets.[Joh.5:39]

God allowed those prophecies to be fulfilled in order to signify that Jesus was the *Messiah* of whom their prophets had spoken, who had come to this world as the Savior.[Joh.19:28-30, 34-37; Acs.5:30-31; 13:23] His life and ministry had fulfilled all that the Law and the priesthood had illustrated.[Luk.24:44-48]

The Perfect Sacrifice
The High Priest

Jesus was God's perfect sacrifice.[Heb.5:9; 10:10-14] His blood was innocent,[Heb.9:14] being *shed...for the remission of our sins.*[Mat.26:28]

He was the High Priest who took His own blood into the Holy of Holies in heaven, into the sacred *presence of God,*[Heb.9:11-12,14,24-26] and His sacrifice was so total and perfect, on our behalf, that God declared (in essence): *It is enough! The sins of all have been justly and fully punished. Nothing more can be required. My Son's death is enough. Now, whoever will believe that He died for them shall be forgiven, ransomed and reborn to the abundant Life that I created him or her for.*

From that day, *The Way* back to God has been open [Heb. 10:18-22] for all who believe.[Joh. 3:16] Men and women can now come back into His sacred presence to live as His friends and partners, never again to be alone.

CHAPTER FIFTY

GOD'S PLAN TO OPEN THE WAY

REMEMBER THE PRIESTHOOD and the sacrifices that were illustrated in the Old Testament; and remember what was accomplished by Jesus Christ through His vicarious death for us on the Cross. It all revealed God's love—His plan to open *The Way* for us to come back into His Holy Presence.

He came to our level, into our realm of human flesh, to open *The Way* for us to re-enter the realm of His presence. This required the punishment of our sins. Since *all had sinned,*[Rom.3:23] and since *the wages of sin is death,*[Rom.6:23] the guilty could not bear their own punishment—and live.

237

So God gave His Son to assume the judgment of our sins in order to clear us of all guilt and condemnation.[Joh.3:16; Rom.8:1]

The Way Back To God

Through Christ's vicarious death on the Cross, He opened up *The Way* back into God's presence. That is why He said, *I am The WAY.*[Joh.14:6]

Those who followed Jesus Christ came to be known as followers of *The Way.*[Acs.19:9, 23]

The great persecutor of early Christians, Saul of Tarsus (known as Paul after his conversion), went about *with authority to arrest any that he found who were of The Way.*[Acs.9:2]

We are told of some who rejected this Gospel of Christ and *spoke evil of The Way.* [Acs.19:9]

The Bible speaks of a great stirring among the people concerning *The Way.*[Acs.19:23]

Another verse speaks of two Christians witnessing to a man about Jesus and what His death on the Cross meant and *they expounded unto him The Way of God.*[Acs.18:26]

In Paul's testimony he told about how he *persecuted The Way unto death.*[Acs.22:4]

In another testimony he said, *After The Way which they call a sect, so serve I…God.*[Acs.24:14]

Why was it called *The Way*?

The book of Hebrews explains, *The Way into the Holy Place [or presence of God] had not yet been made manifest, while the first tabernacle was yet standing.* Heb.9:8 This refers to the *tabernacle* that Moses built in the wilderness Acs.7:44 as a teaching system or *schoolmaster* Gal.3:24-25 concerning God's holiness.

Until our sins were remitted by the death of Jesus Christ and expunged through His shed blood, there was no way that we could be reconciled and restored to live in God's Holy Presence because *it was not possible that the blood of bulls and goats could take away sins.* Heb.10:4

Now The Door Is Open

But Christ came,...not with the blood of goats and calves but with His own blood, and He entered the Holy Place, having obtained eternal redemption for us. Heb.9:11-12

Now this verse makes sense: *Where remission is, there is no more offering for sins.* Heb.10:18

So the results are: *Now we can have boldness to enter into the holiest [the presence of God] by the blood of Jesus, by the new and living Way, which He consecrated for us, through the veil, that is to say, His flesh.* Heb.10:19-20

This new way which the early Christians followed was *The Way* back into God's Holy Presence that was opened by Jesus Christ through His own *blood that was offered...to purge our consciences from dead works to serve the living God.*Heb.9:14 As a result, we can now *have boldness to enter into the holiest by the blood of Jesus.*He.10:19

Paul explains that through *the body of Christ's flesh, through His death, He presents us holy and unblameable and unreproveable in God's sight.*Col.1:22 This is Redemption. This becomes a personal reality from the moment we know it, believe it and embrace Christ as our Lord.

The Awesome Illustration

The opening of *The Way* was illustrated by an historic and miraculous phenomenon that took place inside the Jerusalem temple at the precise hour that Jesus *cried aloud and yielded up the ghost* Mat.27:50 on the Cross: *The veil in the temple was rent in two from top to bottom.*Mar.15:38

Historians tell us that this veil, which separated the people from the Sacred Presence of God in the Holy Place, was woven so thick and of such extraordinary material that it would have required six yoke of oxen pulling on each side to tear it.

Only once a year, the high priest entered this Holy Place of God's presence, with scrupulous caution and prudence because if he had sinned, or if he had erred in his mediatorial role, he would die.Exo.28:35

With the blood of an animal that had been slain on behalf of the sins of the priest and of the people,[Heb.9:7] he entered this awesome sanctuary of the presence of God amidst a cloud of incense to make yearly atonement for the people; *the Holy Ghost signifying by this, that The Way into the holiest of all was not yet made manifest, while as the first tabernacle was yet standing.*[Heb.9:8]

No More Separation

At the very hour that *Jesus cried with a loud voice and yielded up His spirit in death for us,*[Luk.23:46] God's angel descended into the temple at Jerusalem and ripped asunder that forbiding veil of separation. [Mat.27:51] That divine act publicly illustrated that *The Way into the Holy Presence of God was now opened for all, by the redeeming death and blood of Jesus Christ.* [Heb.4:14-16]

With our sins expunged, no further sacrifice would ever be needed.[Heb.10:12-14] *The Way* is open. We can all come boldly into God's presence and live with Him again.

Let us therefore come boldly unto the throne of grace, that we may obtain mercy, and find grace to help in time of need. [Heb.4:16] We have received *grace whereby we may serve God acceptably with reverence and godly fear.*[Heb.12:28]

CHAPTER FIFTY-ONE

IN HIS PRESENCE AGAIN

WE CAN NOW *draw near to God, with a true heart in full assurance.*[Heb.10:22] No one had done this since Adam and Eve left the Garden of Eden.

Now, restored to God's presence, we have confidence. *The blood of Jesus Christ was shed for the remission of our sins* [Mat.26:28] *and where remission is, there is no more offering for sins.*[Heb.10:18]

When a debt has been paid, no more payment can be made because that debt no longer exists. When a crime is punished according to the law, that particular crime cannot be punished again. In the same way, now that our sins have been expunged through the sacrifice of Christ, you and I can live without condemnation or fear of judgment, and come into God's Holy Presence again.

Our punishment has been suffered. Jesus endured it in our place. Now we need never fear God's Holy Presence again. We have been made *holy, unblameable and unreproveable.*[Col.1:22] God took the initiative and redeemed us so that He could legally bring us back to His side. He *so loved us* that He ransomed us from the Destroyer.

The Marvel Of Redemption

Our sins were charged to Christ's account. His righteousness was credited to our account.

The veil that separated us from God's presence is ripped apart. We are now welcome again to fellowship with Him who created us.

That is why *there is therefore now no condemnation to those who are in Christ Jesus.*[Rom.8:1] Jesus said, *We shall not come into condemnation; but we are passed from death unto life.*[Joh. 5:24] Instead of guilt, fear and inferiority, John said that we can now *have confidence toward God.*[1Jo.3:21]

We can now come Home. *The Way* for total restoration of fellowship with our Creator has been opened. Jesus is *The WAY.*[Joh.14:6]

Being justified by faith, we have peace with God through our Lord Jesus Christ.[Rom.5:1]

No More Penalty

We need never again be lonely or feel forsaken or abandoned. *We have a friend who sticks closer than a brother or a sister.*[Pro.18:24] Jesus says, *I will never leave you, nor forsake you.*[Heb.13:5] *Lo, I am with you always, even unto the end of the world.*[Mat.28:20]

Now God says, *I will dwell in you, and walk in you; and I will be your God, and you shall be my people...I will be a Father unto you, and you shall be my sons and daughters, says the Lord Almighty.*[2Co.6:16,18]

You are the children of God by faith in Christ Jesus.[Gal.3:26] *You are no more a servant, but a son or daughter, an heir of God through Christ.*[Gal.4:7]

We are no more strangers and foreigners, but fellow citizens...of the household of God.[Eph.2:19]

Now Jesus says we can *abide in Him, and He will abide in us.*[Joh.15:4] When we do that, *we can ask what we will and it shall be done to us.*[Joh.15:7]

He promises, *If we love Him, we will keep His words: and His Father will love us, and they will both come to us and make their abode with us.*[Joh.14:23]

No More *Off Limits*

The Father's presence is no longer limited to some holy sanctuary. Our sin problem has been settled. We have been given Eternal Life and have become part of His family. We now *abide with Him, and He abides with us.*Joh.15:4

This is the result of God's divine plan of redemption for us.

With the barrier of our sins removed and with the righteousness of Jesus Christ credited to our account, we *can drink from the same cup.*Rev.3:20 We now have the same righteousness that He has.

We Now Share The Same *Life*

His sanctification is ours. We share His abundant Life and the same relationship with God that Jesus has.Gal.4:6-7; Joh.17:21-23 His Father is our Father. His Life is ours. We come into His presence with the same freedom that Jesus has. We are in the Family.Eph.3:14-15; 2Pe.1:4; 1Jo.3:1 We are redeemed.Eph.1:7; Col.1:14 We are Royalty.1Pe.2:9; Rev.1:5-6

We do not cry, beg and plead as though we were poor, unworthy, inferior indigents hoping for small favors from God. We are children of His household with fullness of fellowship and fullness of joy.

At One Again With God

We have found *The Way*. We are not alone. We are acceptable to God through Jesus Christ. *He is the One who made us acceptable to God; He made us pure and holy and gave Himself to purchase our sal-*

vation.[1Co.1:30 LB] We live in daily companionship with Him.

He is the vine, and we are the branches[Joh.15:5] so that we share the same Life source. We are one.

How priceless is this discovery! This is the *Good News*. It is *The MESSAGE That WORKS.*

The Way Forever Open

Fear not: For I am with you; be not dismayed, for I am your God. I will strengthen you; yes, I will help you; yes, I will uphold you with the right hand of my righteousness.[Isa.41:10]

When you pass through the waters, I will be with you; and through the rivers, they shall not overflow you; when you walk through the fire, you shall not be burned.[Isa.43:2]

The Lord Himself does go before you; He will be with you, He will not fail you or forsake you: Fear not, neither be dismayed.[Deu.31:8]

Be strong and of a good courage; be not afraid, neither be dismayed: for the Lord your God is with you.[Jos.1:9] *I will be with you: I will not fail you or forsake you.*[Jos.1:5]

FRIENDSHIP WITH GOD IS RESUMED.

CHAPTER FIFTY-TWO

THE PRAYER-
CONFESSION

AS YOU PRAY this prayer-confession aloud, remember the price that has been paid by Christ to open *The Way* into God's presence.

Draw near with a true heart in full assurance of faith.[Heb.10:22] *His ears are open unto your prayers.*[1Pe.3:12] *Through Christ, you now have access by one Spirit to the Father.*[Eph.2:18]

Say this to Him:

DEAR LORD: I thank you for opening *The Way* for me to approach you without fear. What a comfort to know that you want to walk and talk with me as you did with Adam and Eve in the Garden of Eden!

You are always a friend to the friendless, a companion to the lonely, a defense to those in battle, a shelter to those in danger.

You are always strength to the weak, joy to the sorrowful, help to the helpless, health to the sick, righteousness and peace to the sinful, the source of every supply to the needy, the Savior to the lost.

I am overwhelmed knowing that you long to *make your abode with me*—just as I am.

I THANK YOU for helping me to understand your plan for my salvation. Day and night my heart has longed for you, but I was afraid of your presence. I felt guilty, unworthy and condemned. The best I could hope for was that I might be tolerated as an unworthy supplicant of small favors.

I never knew that *you desired my companionship* like loving parents long to have their children near them.

Even the formalities of religion re-enforced the idea that you were afar off and almost unapproachable. Prayer seemed, at best, only a ritual, with answers unlikely. I was constantly made aware of my sins and of your holiness, and that I could only plead and hope for small favors.

NOW I UNDERSTAND, dear Lord, that you created Adam and Eve to be your friends and companions, but that their rebellion required that they be separated from your holy presence until succeeding generations could learn the

248

sacredness and value of companionship with you.

My heart is overwhelmed to see how you sought a way to remove this wall of separation between us, so that I could come back to your side as your child.

I now understand that the Old Testament is like a *schoolmaster* Gal.3:24 that teaches me the meaning of the Cross of Christ and the sacredness of rapport with you.

You used the old system of animal sacrifices and of human priests to illustrate the sacrifice of your Son as *the Lamb of God who takes away the sins of the world.*Joh.1:29 It teaches me how Christ, as my great High Priest,Heb.2:17; 4:14 took His own blood into the Holy Sanctuary of Heaven and sealed my eternal redemption from sins.Heb.9:12.

NOW I CONFESS that Jesus is *the Lamb of God, slain for my sins.*Joh.1:29; Rev.5:9-12 When you paid my penalty, my debt was absolved, and now nothing stands between you and me. Rom.8:1

You believed that if you would send me the *Good News*, I would respond to your love by repenting and accepting Jesus as my Redeemer.

Oh, yes Lord, I do believe the *Good News*. I do confess you as my Lord and Master and as the High Priest of my life. I do welcome you *to make your ABODE with me.*Joh.14:23

NOW, I ENTER your holy presence to live. The barrier between you and me is gone forever. *The Way* is open for me to live in your presence again.

I am no longer guilty before you. What wonderful words! I am not guilty any more. *You have declared me not guilty!*^{Rom.5:9 LB} My penalty has been paid by my Savior, Jesus Christ!

NOW I HAVE your righteousness. A *new Life* is in me. I am *saved*. You and I are one. Thank you, Lord, for redeeming me. Thank you for sending me this message. Your love dwells in me now. My body is your temple. You have come to make your abode with me. We now drink from the same cup.

You are my defense, my protection, my healing and my peace. You are my righteousness and my happiness. You are the source of Life in me now. You are my health and my strength. You stand against my enemies. When plagues and evil threaten me now, they must deal with you because I am hidden in Christ.

Now I have peace and tranquillity. I have strength and joy. My *FRIENDSHIP WITH YOU IS RESUMED*. Thank you! Amen!

Section VII

Victory Retrieved

◇ 📖 ◇

VICTORY
SUCCESS
THE BEST FOR YOU

GOD REVEALS HIMSELF BY HIS *REDEMPTIVE* NAME, *JEHOVAH-NISSI* TRANSLATED *"THE LORD OUR BANNER."* Exo.17:15 VICTORY IS A *REDEMPTIVE* BLESSING, PAID FOR ON OUR BEHALF AND *IN OUR NAME* BECAUSE *GOD "GIVES US THE VICTORY THROUGH OUR LORD JESUS CHRIST."* 1Co.15:57 BY HIS SACRIFICE ON THE CROSS, HE HAS *"SPOILED PRINCIPALITIES AND POWERS; AND HAS MADE A SHOW OF THEM OPENLY, TRIUMPHING OVER THEM, ... QUICKENING US TOGETHER WITH HIM."* Col.2:15,13

CHAPTER FIFTY-THREE

YOU ARE MADE TO WIN

MEN AND WOMEN were created to be winners. Failure is not God's will. He never wants you or me to bow to the demon of defeat.

Insecurity and uncertainty are not what God planned for us. He does not propose mediocrity. His plan is that we be linked with Him as winners, as victors.

A perpetual conflict is waged around us. Right struggles against wrong. Evil supplants good. Disease encroaches upon health. Lust plots to overthrow love. Subservience obstructs success.

Humanity is caught in the Crossfire of life's battles for achievement. Atheism, cynicism and unbelief usurp the place of faith. Mistrust and dishonesty eat like termites at the foundations of life. Every man and woman needs a source from which to draw strength to win in life's struggle.

Strategies For Conquest

Humanity's adversary, the devil, is relentless. He seeks, by every cunning device, to thwart the success of those who follow Christ.

The Evil One maneuvers his deceptive tactics to swindle God's children out of their rights. He plots to obstruct their relationship with God. He accuses or condemns them in order to destroy their faith. He maligns them with a devastating sense of inferiority and unworthiness. If he fails to make Christians doubt God's promises, he will suggest that biblical provisions are not applicable in their case.

Tactics Of The Destroyer

When people are unaware of God's plan and promises for His children, they become vulnerable to the tactics of the Destroyer, and invariably they succumb to destructive negativism and concepts of failure.

The Christian believer must resist mediocrity and subjugation, because failure is never God's will for His children.

CHAPTER FIFTY-FOUR

WHAT YOU KNOW MAKES THE DIFFERENCE

NEGATIVE BOOKS, impugning sermons and outmoded religious traditions fuse to convince people that defeat is a greater blessing than success. Society is often influenced to believe that submission and surrender are of greater spiritual value than conquering and winning.

Christians are urged to accept inadequacy and indigence and to surrender objectivity. These fatalistic influences can cast an oppressive shadow upon people's lives that triggers demoralizing thoughts, pessimistic speech and defeatest behavior. It is Satan's deadly routine for breeding negativism and humiliation.

Blessings In Disguise?

If people are not vigilant, religious pessimists can have them worshipping at the shrine of defeat, convinced that problems and poverty are "blessings in disguise" sent from the loving Father to teach patience, humility and submission.

The conflict is perpetual. That is why believers must be convinced that God created them to be happy, to be blessed, and to be winners — to succeed!

When Truth Is Not Embraced

What happens to Christians who are unaware of God's redemptive blessings for victory?

Very often, fear dominates, impossibilities evolve, business ventures fail, and dreams are thwarted. People become frightened, irritated, and angry — with themselves and with others. Their words become offensive and hostile. The devil wields his demoralizing influence. They fall into demeaning cycles of disillusionment and confusion. Problems loom and they perceive no solutions.

Satan whispers degrading and destructive thoughts suggesting that God is not concerned about them, that He is perhaps punishing them with failure or defeat because of pride or some other negative tendency. He disturbs their nights, accusing them of shortcomings.

The Deceiver's Age-Old Scheme

The Deceiver has never changed his strategy of temptation and demoralization. His goal is always to cause people to doubt God's promises in the same way that he influenced Adam and Eve to question what God had said to them.

Satan twists the Word of God and preys on human emotions in times of stress. He is relentless in his campaign to destroy faith in God. If he can accomplish that, he knows that people will usually abandon faith in others, and consequently, renounce faith in themselves.

Misery, depression, poverty and failure become the disastrous harvest of this broken confidence.

So WHAT IS THE ANSWER? Must one struggle forever? Can there never be victory? Is the battle never won? Are people doomed to destruction by this calamitous prospect?

No! A thousand times, no! There is victory for you. There is victory for you right now. And you are ready now to step up to a higher level where that victory can become a reality in your life.

The next chapters will help you to embrace the rich redemptive blessings of victory that are already yours in Christ.

CHAPTER FIFTY-FIVE

CHRIST OUR CAPTAIN

JESUS CHRIST IS CALLED *the captain of our salvation.*^{Heb. 2:10} *Salvation* is the all-inclusive term that embraces everything that the Lord accomplished for us in His death on the Cross.

Rescue, safety, deliverance, forgiveness, protection, health, prosperity, preservation, freedom, liberty, peace, righteousness, victory.

Both the Greek and Hebrew languages confirm this all-inclusive scope of what the Bible calls *Salvation.*^{Heb.5:9; 1Pe.1:3-5; Heb.2:3-4; 1Th.5:8-10; Eph.6:17; Acs.4:10-12; Rom.10:10} It is God's abundant living.^{Joh.10:10; Eph.3:20; Tit.3:5-7; 2Pe.1:4, 10-11; 2Co.9:8}

The New *LIFE*

God created you for triumph and for victory — to win in life. Adam and Eve forfeited victorious living when they dishonored and disregarded God's Word in the Garden of Eden.

Salvation is God's New Life Plan by which He restores to us all of the blessings that were forfeited by Adam and Eve's disobedience and lack of faith.[1Co.3:22-23; Joh.1:16; Eph.4:13; Col.1:19; 2:9-10]

Jesus died so that we might live.[Joh.14:19] He took our defeats and gives us His success.[Col.1:13-14; 2Co.2:14; Eph.1:20-21]

Discovery For Victory

✓ **We are no longer** estranged from God, separated from Him by our sins and iniquities.[Isa.59:2] The righteousness of Christ has been imputed to us.[Rom.3:21-22; 1Co.1:30; 2Co.5:21; 1Pe.2:24] *Our Dignity as God's creation is RESTORED.*

✓ **We no longer** live in fear of God, uncertain about our relationship with Him.[Eph.2:12-14,16] He is our Peace, and we rest, confident in His salvation. [Col.1:20-23] *Our Peace with God is RECOVERED.*

✓ **We are no longer** misguided through confusion and wrong decisions.[Psa.32:6-8; 48:14; 73:23-24] *The Lord is our Shepherd,*[Psa.23:1] and He guides us in each detail of life.[Pro. 3:5-6] *Our Signals with Him are REFOCUSED.*

260

✓ **We are no longer** dominated by sickness and disease. The Lord is our *Physician,* our Life.[Exo.15:25; 23:25; Psa.103:3] *Our Health is RENEWED.*

✓ **We are no longer** doomed to live in destitution and need.[Psa.23:1,5; 31:19; 84:11] God is our source of supply.[Phi.4:19; Psa.36:6-9; 89:11] *Our Prosperity, as a member of His Family, is REGAINED.*

✓ **We are no longer** alone and in despair. Jesus Christ is always *with us.*[Mat.28:20; Heb.13:5] He is Present. *Our Friendship with Him is RESUMED.*

✓ **We are no longer** defeated in life's battles. [1Co.15:57; 1Jo.4:4] The Lord is our *victory.*[Psa.18:2; Phi.4:13] We have been lifted from mediocrity to excellence. We are Winners. *Our Victory has been RETRIEVED.*

THESE BLESSINGS AND PROVISIONS are all included in God's gift of salvation. [Heb.2:3] It is His will that we have victory—total victory in every phase of our lives. [Rom.8:37]

Christ's Triumph

Three days after Christ's death on the Cross, *God raised Him from the dead according to the scriptures.* [1Co.15:4] He rose in total victory over our adversary, Satan. [Eph.1:20-22] And when Christ was raised, we *were raised with Him through the faith of*

the operation of God, who raised Him from the dead.
Col.2:12

He said, *Fear not; I am He who lives, and was dead; and, behold, I am alive for evermore...and I have the keys of hell and of death.* Rev.1:17-18

Our New Heritage

Now you can value these Bible statements:

You, being dead in your sins...has He quickened together with Him, having forgiven you all trespasses. Blotting out everything that was against you...He took it out of the way, nailing it to His Cross. And having spoiled principalities and powers, He made a show of them openly, triumphing over them in it.
Col.2:13- 15

Our Language Renewal

You and I can say with Paul: *Like as Christ was raised up from the dead by the glory of the Father, even so we also walk in newness of Life.* Rom.6:4

We can say: *In all these things, we are more than conquerors through Him who loved us.* Rom.8:37 *Thanks be to God, who always causes us to triumph in Christ,* 2Co.2:14 *because if God be for us, who can be against us* Rom.8:31 *for we are dead (to sin) and our lives are hid with Christ in God.* Col.3:3

For the Son of God was manifested, that He might destroy the works of the devil, 1Jo.3:8 *and now we are of*

God...and have overcome (the devil) because greater is He that is in us, than he that is in the world. [1Jo.4:4]

Vulnerable No More

Jesus is our Captain. Our salvation is complete. He died to provide all that we need or desire. His abundant Life is now imparted to us. We have the victory. We are always winners because Christ is our Captain, our Victory, our Life.

Chapter Fifty-Six

Legacy For Living

NOBODY KNOWS, more than Satan himself, all that Jesus Christ accomplished for us in His vicarious death, burial and resurrection.

As long as Satan can obstruct people from knowing what Christ accomplished on their behalf, he can beat them in every encounter. In the Garden of Eden, he caused Adam and Eve to question God's Word [Gen.3:1,4] and as a result, was able to enslave them. He became their master.

Jesus said, *Satan comes not but to steal and to kill and to destroy.*[Joh.10:10]

The Prowling Menace
The Empty Roar

Peter said, *Your enemy, the devil, walks about as a roaring lion, seeking whom he may devour.*[1Pe.5:8] Note the words *whom* – not everyone, and *may* – or we could say, may *not*.

Satan has no power to devour *believers,* nor is he able to devour *at will*. He can only devour those who believe his lies because they do not know the victory that Christ accomplished on their behalf and in their name. They are uninformed so they naively accept Satan's lies as fact.

James said, *Resist the devil, and he will flee from you*.[Jam.4:7] In other words, instead of bowing to his lying suggestions, believers speak in his face the facts of the Gospel, acting on them, and the result is that Satan flees.

That is resisting the devil with God's Word in your testimony,[Rev.12:11] and it puts the enemy to flight.

That is acting on the victory that Christ has won on your behalf and in your name.

Chapter Fifty-Seven

Imagery That Misses The Mark

AN INFINITE LEGACY is bequeathed to Bible believers. God's Word promises, *In all these things we are more than conquerors through Him that loved us.*[Rom.8:37]

No weapon that is formed against us shall prosper; and every tongue that shall rise against us in judgment we shall condemn. This is the heritage of the servants of the Lord, and their righteousness is of me, says the Lord.[Isa.54:17]

The Lucrative Label

Since Bible days, *deceivers, seducers, false teachers, vain talkers,*[2Ti.3:13; 1Ti.1:10;] and *heretics* [2Pe.2:1] have disturbed, confused and disquieted Christians lacking knowledge of what Christ has accomplished for them, can be vulnerable to misguiding voices.

Through worldwide electronic and fiber-optics media, Christians of this generation are obliged to cope with an unprecedented bombardment of *divers and strange doctrines.*[Heb.13:9] Occasionally when I return from ministering in other nations, I am bewildered and at times appalled by concepts that I hear pontificated publicly.

Great emphasis is promulgated about *Spiritual Warfare.* The label has become lucrative for public marketing, motivating countless books, broadcasts, and audio or video cassettes, all of which proliferate in our world.

Warfare That Misses The Target

Spiritual warfare as often presented, misses the objective that Paul had in mind. Teachers and preachers conjure up images of the forces of God (Christians) and the forces of Satan (evil spirits and rulers of darkness) pitted against each other as contending powers that are so nearly equal that the conflict is only won if Christians intercede and pull down enough strongholds. [2Co.10:4]

Intercession is a biblical and valid ministry of prayer, essential in the Church. Paul emphasized it.[Eph.6:18; Phi.4:6;] But he never told Christians to struggle against devils as though they can impede or interdict access to the Heavenly Father or as though evil spirits may possess and rule the lives of believers. These concepts indicate a limited understanding of redemption.

Daniel's Prayer
Hindered For 21 Days

Daniel's experience in the Old Testament is cited as an example of how *rulers of darkness* and *spiritual wickedness in high places* can hinder or impede a believer's prayers from reaching God.

Daniel set himself to pray for twenty-one days, on behalf of his nation. The Bible says that *the prince of the kingdom of Persia withstood* him. Finally, Daniel testifies, that *Michael, one of the chief princes, came to help me,* and told me that *from the first day...your words were heard...but the prince of the kingdom of Persia withstood me twenty-one days* Dan.10:10-13

This example is used to encourage Christians to struggle against the *prince of the powers of the air* and *spiritual wickedness in high places,* as Daniel did. They are told that their prayers may not reach the Throne of God because they may be hindered by emissaries of Satan unless they intercede long enough. Then angels may join in the conflict, as they did for Daniel, so that their prayers can finally be effective.

Not Under The Old Covenant

That was an Old Testament example. When Daniel struggled for those three weeks, Jesus Christ had not yet conquered Satan and his demons. He had not yet wrenched from the Evil One his dominion over people.

In Christ's vicarious death and resurrection, Satan was stripped of authority over believers. [Col.1:12-14; 2:15] The Liar, the Defeated One, has no ability now to interdict the prayers of one of God's children. Jesus says, *Ask and it shall be given you...For **everyone** who asks receives.*[Mat.7:7-8]

Access To God Through Christ

Redemption is a finished work: *Christ being come a high priest...by His own blood, has entered into the holy place, having obtained eternal redemption for us...He is entered...into heaven itself, now to appear in the presence of God for us.*[Heb.9:11-12,24]

Seeing then that we have a great high priest that is passed into the heavens, Jesus the Son of God, let us...therefore come boldly to the throne of grace, that we may obtain mercy, and find grace to help in time of need.[Heb.4:14-16]

No longer may demons impede our prayers to our Heavenly Father. Victory is ours. *And if we know He hears us, whatever we ask, we **know** that we **have** the petitions that we desired of Him.*[1Jo.5:15]

Taking Paul's Words
Out Of Their Original Context

This popular concept of struggling in prayer against evil spirits and powers is based on Paul's counsel to Timothy, to the Ephesians and to the Corinthians.

♦ *Fight the good fight of faith.*[1Ti.6:12]

♦ *Put on the whole armor of God, that you may be able to stand against the wiles of the devil.*

♦ *For we wrestle not against flesh and blood, but against principalities, against powers, against the rulers of the darkness of this world, against spiritual wickedness in high places.* [Eph.6:11-12]

♦ *For the weapons of our warfare are not carnal, but mighty through God to the pulling down of strong holds.*[2Co.10:4]

Paul was not speaking to Christians about spiritual warfare inside the church, within the body of believers. He was writing to encourage them concerning their witness of Christ out in an environment that was hostile to the new Christian "sect" (as society regarded followers of Christ then).

Witnessing In A Belligerent Society
Real *Spiritual Warfare*

Paul was counseling young churches that when they witnessed about the death, burial and resurrection of Jesus Christ, there would be fierce opposition because they were considered a sect that was officially condemned by the Roman government.

Persecution of Christians was common. It was popular to collaborate with officials in locating and arresting them, so they could be hauled off to prison, torture and death, as Paul had done before his conversion.[Acs.9:1-2; 22:4-5; 26:10-11; Gal.1:13]

The situation was so critical that Paul wrote to remind believers that they must be prepared to *fight the good fight of faith,*[1Ti.6:12] and that they would need to *put on the whole armor of God, to stand against Satan's wiles,* because as Christ's witnesses, they were *not wrestling against flesh and blood, but against principalities, powers, rulers of darkness and spiritual wickedness in high places.*[Eph.6:13,12]

Engaged In Warfare
That Is Already Won

Christians who lack knowledge of New Testament culture may misconstrue these statements of Paul, applying them to spiritual warfare among believers, instead of the conflict involved in witnessing to *un*-believers about Christ and His Gospel.

Prayer and intercession for each other in the Body of Christ is vital. James said, *pray one for an-*

other.[Jam.5:16] Paul said, *We that are strong ought to bear the infirmities of the weak.*[Rom.15:1]

But when Paul wrote about *pulling down strongholds*, and *wrestling against principalities, powers and rulers of darkness*, he was not talking about Christians praying for one another in the Body of Christ. He was talking about Christians going out into a dangerous world to bear witness of Jesus Christ at the risk of persecution, arrest, imprisonment, physical torture, and death. That is the warfare *against spiritual wickedness in high places in* which those early believers were engaged. And it is the same today.

Paul wanted to encourage them so he reminded them that Jesus had *spoiled those principalities and powers, that He had made a public show of their defeat, and that He had triumphed over them.*[Col.2:15]

Christ won the victory over Satan's evil influence and now *He gives us the victory.*[1Co.15:57] He *always causes us to triumph.*[2Co.2:14]

What encouragement such words must have been to those precious, beleaguered believers who were sacrificing everything and risking their lives to witness about Christ during that epoch of insidious persecution!

Witnessing With Courage

To *fight the fight of faith* means to identify with Jesus Christ in His triumph over Satan. Christian believers need not struggle to conquer an enemy that Christ has already defeated. They must carry their witness with boldness and with courage, believing that Jesus, who triumphed over Satan, is at work in them, and that He is *greater in the believer than Satan is in the world.*[1Jo.4:4]

Real spiritual warfare is not fighting demon spirits in the Church or in other Christians. Those weaknesses or influences of the enemy are to be *overcome,* not *cast out.*

Satan's oppressing spirits will relentlessly tempt and pressure Christians, deceiving them, tricking them, diverting them by delusions and chicanery. He will oppress their bodies with pain and sickness and their minds with negative and doubtful thoughts that contradict God's Word. The believer's recourse is to *resist the devil (with the facts of the Word of God), and he will flee from you.*[Jam.4:7]

That is why Paul said: *Cast down imaginations, and every high thing (thought) that exhalts itself against the knowledge of God, and bring into captivity every thought to the obedience of Christ.*[2Co.10:5]

Evil Spirits That Cannot Be *Cast Out*

A believer cannot cast out evil spirits that sow negative and doubtful thoughts in the minds of Christians. A believer cannot cast out spirits of discouragement or fear or doubt. These symptoms are the result of one's thoughts — negative thoughts that contradict redemptive fact. Such "spirits" cannot be *cast out*. They must be *overcome* through a resolve to embrace the facts of the Word of God instead of doubting them.

Christians cannot run to their believing friends when they feel discouraged or frightened or oppressed and ask them to cast those evil spirits out of them.

Paul was urging believers to deal with those negative influences themselves. They concern people's thoughts. Discouragement and fear are the result of thoughts.

When Christians choose to think wrong thoughts, they become discouraged or frightened. Everyone has the right of choice. You can choose to change your thoughts. Paul said, in essence, "You don't need to run to stronger believers, asking them to cast out the spirits of discouragement or fear. Your part is to *bring into captivity every thought to the obedience of Christ*. You cast down fearful imaginations — every *thought that exhalts itself against the knowledge of God*.

Thinking God's Thoughts

Analyze your thoughts. If they contradict the facts of redemption, then simply change your thoughts. Think redemptive thoughts. Think of what God says. Remember it. Ponder it. Rejoice in it. Talk it. Communicate it. Believe it. And act on it. Discouragement will dissipate like a fog in the sunshine.

Wherefore lift up the hands which hang down, and the feeble knees; And make straight paths for your feet, lest that which is lame be turned out of the way; but let it rather be healed. Follow peace with all people, and holiness, without which no one shall see the Lord: Looking diligently lest anyone fail of the grace of God; lest any root of bitterness springing up trouble you, and thereby others be defiled. Heb.12:12-15

Finally, brothers and sisters, whatever things are true, whatever things are honest, whatever things are just, whatever things are pure, whatever things are lovely, whatever things are of good report; if there be any virtue, and if there be any praise, think on these things. Phi.4:8

And be not conformed to this world: but be transformed by the renewing of your mind, that ye may prove what is that good, and acceptable, and perfect, will of God. Rom.12:2

❖ ❖ ❖

THIS ENTIRE BOOK is written to help you do exactly that. Each of your basic seven needs are provided by God's seven redemptive provisions, provisions paid for by Christ's death for you. As you grasp them, embrace them, speak them, and act on them, God will confirm them in your life, and you will experience victory.

To be a winner with God, identify with Christ's victory over Satan. When He won, you won. You are in Him. He is in you. *Now He always causes you to triumph.* [2Co.2:14]

CHAPTER FIFTY-EIGHT

WARFARE NOT WITCHCRAFT

I HAVE OFTEN VISITED pagan villages in nations abroad, observing heathen rituals, dances, and ceremonies. (See my booklet, *I Witnessed A Pagan Sacrifice*.)

I have talked with many national converts from *non*-Christian religions who have told me about local superstitions. The principle concern of pagan villagers is the appeasement of evil spirits which they believe are the agents of spiritual, physical and material evil. They engage in vain attempts to pacify these "demons" by blood sacrifices and the mediatorial incantations of priests or witchdoctors.

Witchcraft Among *Non*-Christians

Non-Christian village people engage mediums at great cost to act on their behalf, offering sacrifices with rituals to exorcise evil spirits from their homes, villages, markets and businesses.

Having witnessed these practices abroad, I am disturbed when I return to my country and hear Christians waging "spiritual warfare" and "pulling down strongholds," presuming to drive out evil spirits from believers or places of worship or residences or businesses or areas. They imagine themselves "wrestling against principalities and powers" which they visualize as pressuring or over-powering or oppressing or possessing Christian believers. To me, this resembles what pagans abroad do, except that they use different vocabulary.

Christians who espouse ideas like these have gullibly embraced a concept of spiritual warfare that is incompatible with redemptive truth and inconsistent with what Paul was addressing.

IN THE NEXT CHAPTERS, we will look at the meaning of Paul's statements to Timothy, to the Ephesians and to the Corinthians. Perhaps some of the confusion—or even delusion about prayer and spiritual warfare can be alleviated.

CHAPTER FIFTY-NINE

INTERCESSORY PRAYER PLUS WITNESSING ACTION

WHEN CHRISTIANS IMAGINE demonic powers arrayed against them in spiritual conflict, and they believe that their warfare against these principalities requires long intercessions, then they are discrediting the victory that Christ won through His death and resurrection.

To visualize Satan's power pitted against God's people in a struggle that may be lost if Christians do not wrestle long enough, negates Christ's victory and gives undue credit to the enemy.

Two Concepts Of Prayer

Two notions about prayer contradict the truths of redemption.

1) The belief that Christians must wrestle against *principalities, powers and the rulers of the darkness of this world* within the Church. That is not where these principalities and rulers exist unless Christians concede place to them. Satan has no right to impose his destructive works in the lives of believers who have been delivered out of his domain and are *translated into the kingdom of God's dear Son.*[Col.1:13]

2) The belief that by prayer and intercession, Christians can wage warfare against Satan and bring down his power in the *un*-converted world where he has the right to rule his own subjects. God never imposes His dominion—not over people, not over demons, not over Satan. Jesus did not—could not. Believers cannot.

Limits In The Dark World

First, we will consider what authority Christians have in the world of darkness.

Remember that, in the lives of believers, Jesus Christ is Lord. The only power that Satan can wield against Christians is the power that they concede to him. He has none of his own.

But in the *un*-converted world, Satan is the legal ruler. The only power that Christians can wield on his territory, among his subjects, is to witness to them of the Gospel. When that is done, then Satan cannot interdict the right of choice of his subjects. They can choose to believe the Gospel or to reject it. And if they choose to believe it, then Satan must relinquish his rule over them

By the same principle, Christians are obliged to respect the decisions of those who do not embrace the Gospel. That is why they cannot enter Satan's territory and *impose* God's will on people. If *un*-believers reject the Good News, the Christian has no authority to impose Christ's deliverance. The power that saves people is the power of the knowledge of the Gospel.^{Rom.1:16}

Even Christ Himself *could do no mighty work,* ^{Mar.6:5} in His home town of Nazareth *because of their unbelief.*^{Mat.13:58} And when Jesus looked over the city of Jerusalem, He lamented, *O Jerusalem,... how often I would have gathered your children together, as a hen gathers her brood under her wings, but you would not!* ^{Luk.13:34}

God never *imposes* His rule. He did not in the Garden of Eden. He did not in the ministry of Jesus. He did not in the early church. He does not now. He *offers* His salvation as a gift. The believer's part is to publicize God's offer, and the hearer's choice is to accept or to reject the gift.

When God created people, He gave them a free will and He never violates that right of choice. Paul said, *To whom you yield yourselves servants to obey, his servants you are to whom you obey; whether of sin unto death, or of obedience unto righteousness?* Rom.6:16 Peter said, *Of whom a person is overcome, of the same is he or she brought into bondage.*2Pe.2:19 The Living Bible says it like this: *For a person is a slave to whatever [or whoever] controls him or her.*

That is why Christians cannot reform people by casting evil spirits out of them. What they *can* do is teach God's Word to people, then people can embrace or reject His truths. They can conform their thinking to God's plan and resist the enemy, *overcoming* the temptations of their flesh, or they can chose to ignore God's way. They have the right of choice and no one can *impose* God's Good Life Agenda.

Believers cannot cast out the "spirit of gluttony" from someone who is obese from over-eating or the "spirit of drunkenness" from someone who consumes alcoholic drinks. These destructive habits are to be *overcome*, not *cast out*. *Be not overcome of evil, but overcome evil with good,*Ro.12:21 is Paul's counsel. He never suggested that we cast evil habits out of people. They are to be overcome.

The Power Of The Gospel

Demons know the Gospel and its power. They know that their only power of resistance is to prevent the Gospel from coming to the attention of their subjects because, if the *un*-converted come to *know the truth, the truth will make them free.*Joh.8:32

We do not win lost souls by interceding and struggling in prayer to defeat evil spirits and to bring down Satan's strongholds in their lives. We win over the principalities of darkness by giving to people the delivering truths of the Gospel. That is the power that pulls down Satan's strongholds and that brings salvation to the lost.

Prayer Plus Witnessing

Prayer and intercession are essential to the believer's preparation and ministry. But witnessing is the Christian's action. Nothing substitutes for action.

Un-converted people who are ignorant of the Gospel will not be brought to Christ through the intercession of believers. They can only be *saved through faith.*Eph.2:8 That faith comes through *hearing the Word of God.* Rom.10:17 They hear that *Word* when believers share the Gospel with them.

Paul asked, *How can they call on Him in whom they have not believed? and how shall they believe in*

Him of whom they have not heard? and how shall they hear without a preacher [or messenger]? Rom.10:14

Prayer And Intercession

Paul spoke of *helping together by prayer.*2Co.1:11 He was on the front lines and needed the Christians to *help* him in prayer. What for? He said, *That the Word of the Lord might have free course* 2Th.3:1 and not be hindered by the rulers of darkness or rejected by the people.

Paul did not engage the Christians to pull down the *strongholds of the rulers of darkness* by intercession. They had no authority to order Satan's surrender and *impose* the Christian faith. To bring Christ's Salvation to the *un*-converted, Paul knew that he must confront the Enemy on his own territory and inform his subjects of the Gospel which *is the power of God unto salvation.*Rom.1:16

Paul knew that if he did that effectively, under the anointing of the Holy Spirit, his Gospel witness would have *free course* and the people would hear it and believe it. When they did that, Satan's *strongholds* would be *pulled down* and his rule over their lives would be ended because Satan cannot hold captives against their will to receive Jesus Christ as Lord.

Chapter Sixty

Options: Believe Or Not Believe

After Christ's Resurrection, believers went forth as His witnesses,^{Acs.1:8; 2:32; 3:15; 4:33; 5:32} and *many of them which heard the Word **believed**; and the number of them was about five thousand.*^{Acs.4:4} Those five thousand people exercised their right of choice. They chose to believe the Good News when they had the opportunity to hear it.

They did not become believers because someone defeated the *principalities and powers of darkness* over them by intercession. No doubt those early believers prayed and interceded, ^{Acs.4:24-31}

but their praying was objective. They were praying for *boldness to speak the Word of the Gospel.*[v.29] They prayed, but they also *spoke the Word of God with boldness,* [v.31] among *un*-believers.

Response To Christ's Witnesses

Philip went into the *un*-believing city of Samaria and publicly told the people about Christ. His message evidently had *free course* [2Th.3:1] in the city. I imagine the apostles and believers at Jerusalem were on their knees praying that Philip's witness would be unhindered in Samaria.

The believers had been *scattered abroad because of the great persecution against the church, and they had gone everywhere preaching the Word.*[Acs.8:1,4] Philip had been one of them, and he went to Samaria. The people there **believed** *Philip preaching the things concerning the kingdom of God, and the name of Jesus Christ.*[Acs.8:12]

The followers of Christ did not stay in the Upper Room to *wrestle against the principalities, powers and the rulers of darkness* that hung over Samaria, *pulling down Satan's stronghold* from over that city.

To deliver Satan's captives in Samaria, the message and witness of the Gospel had to be taken to them. The Samaritans exercised their right of choice and believed. Satan could not prevent them. His power was invalid before Gospel truth then, and it is invalid today.

Some *Believed* — Some *Believed Not*

Paul went to Thessalonica to preach Christ. *They received the Word with all readiness of mind... and many of them believed.*[Acs.17:11-12] Prayer and intercession at Jerusalem would not have succeeded alone. A believer needed to go and give the Gospel to the people. Satan could not prevent them from choosing Christ when they heard the Good News. The people believed. They were delivered. The Gospel did its work.

Paul went to Athens and was *pressed in his spirit to testify that Jesus was the Christ* [Acs.18:5] But he could not prevail against the will of the people. There *they opposed and blasphemed* Paul's witness so *he departed.*[v.7] Christians cannot impose God's deliverance upon those who do not choose to believe. Demons, angels and people all have their right of choice.

Paul went to another house to witness of Christ. There, a *synagogue ruler believed on the Lord with his house; and many of the Corinthians, hearing, believed.*[Acs.18:8]

Paul witnessed of Christ in another town, but his words were rejected and he had no power to impose God's blessings against their will. *When divers were hardened, and believed not, but spake evil of that way...Paul departed from them.*^{Acs.19:9} That was all he could do. They chose to reject Christ.

Where Paul gave the Gospel and people chose to believe it, salvation came. But where they rejected it, Paul moved on. Intercession could not impose change in people against their own will.

Soon after Paul was rejected, he witnessed to some other people *and many of them* **believed,** *and confessed, and shewed their deeds.*^{Acs.19:18}

Another Bible verse says that *some* **believed** *the things which were spoken, and some* **believed not.** ^{Acs.28:24} That is what Jesus said would take place: *Those who* **believe** *shall be saved; those who* **believe not** *shall be damned.*^{Mar.16:16}

While Paul was in Rome under house arrest, prior to his execution, *many came to his lodging to whom he expounded and testified...concerning Jesus... and some* **believed**...*and some* **believed not.**^{Acs.28:23-24}

THAT WAS HOW the Church began. Nothing has changed. Prayer must be accompanied by witnessing action. *Un*-believers are saved when believers take the message of the Gospel to the enemy's territory, getting the ear of as many as possible, *persuading them,* as Paul did,^{Acs.19:8; 28:23} about Christ.

CHAPTER SIXTY-ONE

VICTORIOUS PRAYER

FOR DAISY AND ME it required over a year for us to reform our prayer lives after we learned about Satan's defeat. Because of our traditional manner of praying, we found ourselves interceding for blessings that God had already promised and provided.

It was difficult for us to conform our prayer life to the facts of redemption. We came to realize that we did not need to intercede for God to keep His promise, nor for Him to give us blessings or gifts that He already offers. Then what were we to pray for? We struggled through the inconsistencies of many traditions in order to conform our prayer lives to biblical, redemptive facts.

Rapport With God

As we grasped faith by reading God's word, then we had to conform our praying to what we had learned. We no longer needed to beg and plead for blessings already provided. As we turned our pleading into thanksgiving, we learned a greater depth in prayer than we have ever known before.

We discovered that intercessory prayer is not begging and pleading before God for His divine favors. Prayer and supplication is drawing life from His presence.

✓ It is communion with our Father.

✓ It is harmonizing our plans with His plans.

✓ It is pondering what His Word says about our ideas and conforming our concepts to His.

✓ It is tuning our spirits and emotions to His Holy Spirit and to His Word.

✓ It is pouring our hearts out before Him.

✓ It is attuning our love with His love for witnessing to a despairing and confused world.

✓ It is worshipping Him for all that He is and for all that He has provided for humanity.

✔ It is thanking Him for His gifts and callings.

✔ It is pondering His attitude toward people.

✔ It is aligning our thinking, our emotions, our plans, and our minds with His.

✔ It is absorbing faith and hope and love from His person, worshipping Him in fellowship.

✔ It is drinking from His Spirit.

✔ It is bidirectional fellowship, pouring out our thoughts and dreams before Him, then listening to the response of His Word and of His Spirit.

✔ It is praying for the needs of fellow-believers and ministers.

✔ It is absorbing God's guidance and wisdom for witnessing of Christ to others in an effective way.

✔ It is so much more than pleading and begging Him for favors. It is life with Him in *the now*.

Preparation In Prayer

Before entering the devil's terrain with the message and witness of the Gospel, we prepare ourselves by prayer and intercession so that *the Word of the Lord might have free course* 2Th.3:1 and so that we will present the Good News in ways that will be convincing and that will be received by people.

We condition our spirits for effective ministry by praying, by pondering His word, by reflecting on His plan, by rethinking His objectives, by remembering His defeat of Satan, by contemplating the Holy Spirit's power in our lives until we are confident that our Gospel witness will be with power to break the grip of Satan over his captives.

We share the Good News with faith and courage, with hope and love, knowing that we are transmitting the Person and the Spirit of Jesus Christ among Satan's captives with the same anointing that rested upon Jesus.[Luk.4:18]

Like Paul, we know that some will *believe* and some will *not believe*, but we pray and intercede before God, consecrating our vessel to Him so that we will *give no offense in any thing, that the ministry be not blamed.*[2Co.6:3]

We pray. We intercede. We take time to ponder our calling, our position, our power, our rights, our mandate, our reasons for believing. We enter the enemy's terrain with full knowledge of who we are, rejecting and resisting every deceitful tactic of Satan that denigrates us or that contradicts redemptive truth. That is the way that we *fight the good fight of faith.*

Advancing the Gospel message of Christ to individuals or to multitudes, *we wrestle against principalities, powers and rulers of the darkness of this world,* and wherever the Gospel is believed, the *strongholds of Satan are pulled down* in people's lives. Captives are delivered from *the power of darkness, and are translated into the kingdom of our God.*[Col.1:13]

That is the mission of the Church corporately and of every Christian individually. Christ *gives us the victory,*[1Co.15:57] because *this is the victory that overcomes the world, even our faith.*[1Jo.5:4] We win the victory over the power and deception of Satan wherever we can *persuade* [2Co.5:11; Gal.1:10] people to hear and believe the message of Christ.

NOW WE SHALL address the other concept of prayer that ignores Christ's victory over Satan. It is Christians imagining that they are "wrestling against principalities, powers and the rulers of the darkness of this world" within the church, among believers in the Body of Christ. It is believers imagining that they are exorcising evil spirits from other Christians.

This perspective of "spiritual ministry" is contrary to the Gospel and exposes a lack of knowledge concerning redemption.

CHAPTER SIXTY-TWO

FABLES AND FANTASIES

A BIG PART OF Paul's letters were written to young churches who were bombarded by heretical and confusing doctrines promulgated by teachers antagonistic to Paul's revelation of redemption.

God And Devils
Do Not Co-Habit

Christian believers cannot be both Christ-possessed and demon-possessed. Our Lord does not cohabit with evil spirits. God did not in the Garden of Eden. Christ does not in the lives of Christians today.

Followers of Christ who believe that they are possessed by evil spirits have been influenced by teachings inconsistent with redemptive truth. And that is not a new misconception.

Philosophies And Vain Talkers

The apostle Paul talked of *doctrines of men.*[Col.2:22] He said, *some would give heed to...doctrines of devils.*[1Ti.4:1] The writer of Hebrews urged that believers *be not carried about with divers and strange doctrines.*[Heb.13:9]

Paul spoke of some who are *proud, knowing nothing...destitute of the truth.*[1Ti.6:4-5] He said that some people *turn their ears from truth to fables.*[2Ti.4:4] He mentioned *vain talkers and deceivers,...who subvert whole houses, teaching things which they ought not, for filthy lucre's sake.*[Tit.1:10-11]

He warned against *false prophets and false teachers who...with feigned words make merchandise of people.*[2Pe.2:1-3]

Why Deception Proliferates

From the beginning of the Church, strange and unsettling doctrines have circulated among Christians. And in this generation, they proliferate because of electronic and laser media that give pontificators of these misconstrued theories the ears of millions.

In this section of *The MESSAGE That WORKS,* we are expounding the redemptive provision of spiritual *VICTORY* — "redemptive" because it is revealed by the redemptive name of God (Jehovah-Nissi) — "redemptive" because it is the victory that has been bought and paid for by Jesus Christ, *who redeemed us to God through His blood.*[Rev.5:9]

CHAPTER SIXTY-THREE

THREE QUESTIONS ABOUT SPIRITUAL WARFARE

THERE ARE THREE essential issues about "spiritual warfare" (as it has been labeled) that need to be understood. These issues, discussed in the next chapters, will provide Christian believers with a better focus and a clearer perspective of prayer and intercession as Paul counseled.

A Conquered Foe
Or a Menacing *"Pro"*

Warfare implies either defeat or victory. God never planned His children for defeat. Paul said,

Thanks be to God who gives us the victory.[1Co.15:57] He said, *Thanks be to God who ALWAYS causes us to triumph.*[2Co.2:14] And he asked: *If God be for us, who can be against us?*[Rom.8:31] Our enemy is a conquered foe. Believers must never forget that redemptive fact.

Many Christians are so enamored by visualizing their conquest of *principalities, powers, rulers of darkness, and spiritual wickedness in high places* that they ignore the fact that Christ has already won this war.

Real Spiritual Warfare

Our Lord has equipped us with what is necessary for total victory as we take His message to the *un*-converted, delivering slaves from Satan's captivity. That is our mandate as Christ's followers. *The Spirit of the Lord God is upon us because He has anointed us to communicate the Gospel.*[Luk.4:18] That is every believer's mission and mandate. It is what real spiritual warfare is all about.

Each Christian's calling is to give witness of the Gospel among the captives of the rulers of darkness in this world. We seek to get their attention so that we can inform them of the Good News. That way, they have a chance to discover what Satan has blinded them from. When they hear it, they can believe it and be delivered and *translated into the kingdom of God's dear Son.*^{Col.1:13} Or they can choose not to believe it.

That is the struggle in which believers must *fight the fight of faith* and for which they must *put on the whole armor of God.*

So our purpose in these next chapters of *The MESSAGE That WORKS* is to examine these three essential issues:

1. What the *Fight of Faith* IS.

2. What the *Fight of Faith* is AGAINST.

3. What the *Armor of God* IS.

These are the essential issues which the believer must know, embrace, trust and act on in order to minister the Gospel successfully to *un*-believers.

Christians who have espoused the foreign ideas of evil spirits in believers' lives, residences, businesses, or places of worship, are people who have not distinguished *fact* from *fiction* concerning the three fundamental issues that we are ready to elucidate in the next chapters.

Chapter Sixty-Four

What The Fight Of Faith IS

Part 1 (Issue No. 1)

FAITH - Believing God's Word
Not Satan's Wiles

PAUL TOLD US to *fight the good fight of faith.*
1Ti.6:12 This is our only fight—the *faith*-fight. It
means that we are to fight to believe what God
says despite voices, imaginations, messages, circumstances, concepts, information or any other
thing, actual or illusory, that contradicts His
Word.

John says, *This is the victory that overcomes the world, even our faith.*[1Jo.5:4] Faith in what? Faith in what God's Word says—faith in the victory of Christ over *all the works of the devil.*[1Jo.3:8]

To *fight the good fight of faith* does not mean to imagine evil spirits beleaguering or harassing Christians so that they must do battle against those spirits as pagans do. That would disclaim or discredit Christ's victory.

The *Believer's* Ministry

In the *non*-converted world, demon spirits have authority to rule, to enslave, to destroy, to steal, and to kill.

Christians do not have authority to extricate *un*-converted people from enslavement to Satan, against their *un*-converted will. But what believers can do is to give the Gospel to the *un*-converted. If they hear it and respond to it, if they repent of their sins and receive Jesus, then those *rulers of darkness* can no longer subjugate them because Christ sets them free by the power of His Gospel when He is embraced as their Lord and Master.

When people believe the Gospel and receive Jesus Christ as their Lord and Savior, evil spirits cannot cohabit with the Lord Jesus. Paul said, *If any one is in Christ, he or she is a new creature: old things are passed away; all things are become new.*

That person is reconciled to God by Jesus Christ. 2Co.5:17-18 Satan's dominion is ended.

The Lord said to Paul, following his conversion, *I have appeared to you to make you a minister and a witness...and now I send you to the Gentiles (the un-converted)...to open their eyes, and to turn them from darkness to light* Acs.26:16-18 Every Gospel believer, both male and female, is chosen by Christ to be His witness in whatever way he or she is inspired to represent Him to *un*-converted people.

When *un*-believers turn from Satan to God, they receive a glorious heritage by faith in Christ. Acs.26:18 Satan's authority over their lives is abrogated. They are *delivered out of his power, and are translated into the kingdom of God's dear Son, in whom they have redemption through His blood, even the forgiveness of sins.* Col.1:13-14

CHAPTER SIXTY-FIVE

WHAT THE FIGHT OF FAITH IS

PART 2 (ISSUE No. 1)

FAITH–Identifying With Christ

FAITH IS BELIEVING that when Jesus, *the captain of our salvation,*[Heb.2:10] *spoiled principalities and powers,*[Col.2:15] we did too. Faith means that we identify with Him in all of His redemptive ministry on our behalf.

When Christ died, we died with Him. *I have been crucified with Christ,*[Gal.2:20] *united with Him in the likeness of His death.*[Rom.6:5]

When Jesus was raised from the dead, *He raised us up with Him, and made us to sit with Him in heavenly places.*[Eph.2:6]

Identified In Redemption

We were *crucified* with Christ.[Gal.2:20] We *died* with Him.[Rom.6:8] We were *buried* with Him.[Rom.6:4] We were *justified* with Him.[Rom.3:24; 5:1] We were *made alive* with Him.[1Co.15:22] We *conquered Satan* with Him.[Rom.6:6-8] We were *raised together* with Him. [Eph.2:5-6] Now we *live* with Him.[2Co.13:4; Gal.2:20] He is in us and we are in Him.[Joh.17:21, 23] Satan and his evil spirits have lost their dominion over us as believing followers of Christ.[1Jo.4:4: Rom.6:14; 1Jo.5:18]

When we believe the Gospel and embrace Christ as our Lord, we become one with Him. Peter says, *We become partakers of His divine nature.*[2Pe.1:4] John says, *Greater is He who is in us, than he [Satan and his evil forces] who is in the [nonconverted] world.*[1Jo.4:4]

CHAPTER SIXTY-SIX

WHAT THE FIGHT OF FAITH IS

PART 3 (ISSUE NO. 1)

FAITH—Embracing Christ's Victory

PAUL WAS WRITING to believers who were involved as Christ's witnesses *publicly, and from house to house.*[Acs.20:20] They witnessed amidst a hostile environment, under the threat of arrest, imprisonment, beatings, torture and death. That was the kind of government and society under which they lived and represented their Lord.

Their warfare was not against evil powers within the Body of Christ — in the lives of believers. Their warfare was outside the Church, out amidst a hostile society, that regarded them as members of the malignant sect of a dead "egomaniac" from Nazareth.

The *Fight of Faith* In A Hostile World

Paul said, *You were sometimes darkness, but now you are light in the Lord: walk as children of light:* [Eph.5:8] Be witnesses. We do not fight this defeated foe on our terrain where Jesus is Lord. We are redeemed. But we fight Satan on his territory, out where he rules the minds and lives of people.

We fight to make known the Good News among Satan's slaves. We fight to penetrate his curtain of darkness, to get the attention of *un*-believers, to make our message known to them, and to convince them of the Gospel.

The believer's ministry is reporting and witnessing of Christ's death, burial, resurrection and Life. It is making known the significance of those events to anyone who will *only believe.*[Acs.1:8; 5:32] Those early followers of Christ did that against overwhelming odds. Their witness seemed like *foolishness*[1Co.1:18] to *un*-believers of their era. It sounded incredible to society.

The Christian Message—*Foolishness*

The people of Paul's period had been convinced that *Christ's disciples had come by night, and had*
306

stolen His body while the guards at the sepulcher slept. Mat.28:13 The resurrection was considered a false claim heralded by *unlearned and ignorant* Acs.4:13 followers of the mystic from Nazareth. *The preaching of the Cross was [regarded as] foolishness* 1Co.1:18 to the people of that era.

The Christian's ministry is to spread the message of the liberating Gospel throughout the world of spiritual wickedness, fighting by faith against principalities and powers, standing against Satan's wiles and crafty maneuvers. To do that with success, they must *put on the whole armor of God.* Eph.6:11

Christ Confirms His Gospel

We know, by experience, what it means to *fight the good fight of faith*, sharing the Gospel with the *non*-converted world. We know what it means to stand against the *wiles of Satan* and to *wrestle against those principalities and powers.*

And we know, by experience, that *the Gospel is the power of God* Rom.1:16 because as we have proclaimed it to multitudes in nearly eighty nations, it has always brought salvation, miraculous healing and new Life to those who believe it and embrace Christ.

I could recount thousands of stories of individuals who have been lifted out of despair and who have come back from the dead, spiritually, in our meetings during the last half of the twentieth century. We place on record our witness that our Lord does *confirm* His Gospel.^{Mar.16:20}

Peter reminded us that *Jesus of Nazareth was approved of God by miracles, wonders and signs.*^{Acs.2:22}

Christ promises, *I will never leave you nor forsake you.*^{Heb.13:5} *Lo, I am with you always, to the end of the world.*^{Mat. 28:20} He won the victory over Satan, and now *He causes us to triumph.*^{2Co.2:14}

CHAPTER SIXTY-SEVEN

WHAT THE FIGHT OF FAITH IS

PART 4 (ISSUE No. 1)

FAITH—The Right of *Choice*

WHEN PAUL SAID to *fight the good fight of FAITH,* he never intended for Christians to imagine evil spirits disturbing Christ's followers or dominating members of God's Royal Family. On the believer's terrain, Satan has no authority.

When God created people, He gave them a free will, a right of choice, which He never violates. He said, *I set before you Life and good, death and evil, blessing and cursing: choose Life, that both you and your seed may live.*[Deu.30:15-19] They could choose Life and blessing, or death and cursing. Whatever they chose was what they would experience.

Adam and Eve, though created in God's image, were never obligated to respect His ways and His Word. They were never forced to believe what He said. And they made a tragic choice. They believed Satan rather than God.

Although Christians are rescued out of the darkness of Satan's domain, they are still free to choose whom they want to believe, and Satan never stops trying to influence them to question God and to choose *evil and death.*

It is a *fight of faith* to believe God's Word when circumstances or voices contradict it. This struggle never ends. Satan never slackens in his efforts to harass and deceive God's people.

Oppression Or Possession

If Christians choose to question or doubt what Christ said or did for them, they annul His blessings and open the door to Satan's influence. The enemy only has power in a Christian's life when it is conceded to him by doubting or questioning the facts of Christ's redemptive work.

Satan cannot possess believers because they are Christ-possessed. But by influencing them to question God's Word, he can *oppress* them.

The Dilemma Of Sickness

That explains why Christians sometimes suffer disease and pain even though Christ bore those maladies for them. Satan is the oppressor. He pressures believers, attacking them, seeking to wound or limit or handicap them physically in order to prevent or divert them from witnessing.

Sickness is an oppression that affects the physical bodies of Christians. While Satan cannot possess their spirits, because they are *redeemed to God by Christ's blood,*[Rev.5:9] he may oppress their physical houses, causing pain and suffering, impeding or obstructing their witness of Christ. Sickness is the *oppression of the devil.*[Acs.10:38]

Rebuking The *Spirit Of Infirmity*

Ministering to sick people, we might rebuke the *spirits of infirmity* [Luk.13:11] sent from Satan to oppress the bodies of believers, commanding them to leave. This does not mean that we are casting evil spirits out of believers. We are contending against an *oppression* that has assaulted the physical houses in which Christians live.

If your residence were infected by termites, you might call a pest-control company to spray your house. They would not spray *you*. The termites would not be in *you* but they would be destroying the house in which you dwelled.

In the same way, sickness might assault your physical body. It is the enemy's oppression. Following Christ's example, we would rebuke it in His name because it has no right to destroy a believer's body. We would not be casting an evil spirit out of you; we would be dealing with the Enemy's *oppressing infirmity* that affected your *physical body*. We would have authority to do that because *Christ Himself took our infirmities, and bare our sicknesses.*Mat.8:17 He bore our diseases so that we need not bear them.

The Bible says, *Jesus went about healing all who were oppressed of the devil.*Acs.10:38 Sickness is the enemy's oppression—not possession. Evil spirits cannot possess Christian believers, but they oppress their physical houses or their minds, suggesting thoughts and imaginations that *exhalt themselves against the knowledge of God.*2Co.10:5

Christian believers are taught by Paul to fight the faith-fight, resisting the devil's lies and maneuvers, choosing to believe what God says instead of what Satan lies about, and when they do that, Christ and His life in them brings cure and health.

If Christians choose to believe the symptoms of Satan's oppressive sickness more than they believe in God's redemptive provision of healing, then sickness gains the ascendancy. This is not because God wills it. It is because Christians are free to choose in whom and in what they believe.

The Enemy's Only Access – *Choice*

Christians will never be free of Satan's wiles, devices or strategies to try to make them question or doubt God's Word. Those tactics are the enemy's only access to tempt and defraud God's people. If he can persuade them to question God's Word, only then can he prevail against them. His approach is the same as it was in the Garden of Eden; that is, he must convince people to question God in order to open the way for his destructive work.

In the same way, when Christians bear witness of the Gospel in the world of *spiritual wickedness in high places,* seeking to persuade people to accept Christ, they have no authority to release Satan's captives from his domain against their will.

What believers *can* do is inform *un*-believers of the Gospel. Then the *un*-converted can exercise their own free will, their right of choice. They can choose Life and live, or they have the right to reject it and die.

This is very important for Christian believers to understand. Our *right of choice* is the fundamental issue in both God's family and in *un*-believers.

✧ ✧ ✧

CHAPTER SIXTY-EIGHT

WHAT THE FIGHT OF FAITH IS

PART 5   (ISSUE NO. 1)

FAITH—Devils Are No Problem

WHEN JESUS SENT His followers *into all the world to preach [communicate and express] the Gospel to every creature,*^{Mar.16:15} the first sign that He promised would confirm their ministry as believers was essentially: You will have no problem with the devil. His actual words were: *In my name you shall cast out devils.*^{Mar.16:17}

Christ assured His followers that when they go out into the world of darkness to witness about Him, evil influences might rise up against them but Christ's Holy Spirit would be with them and in them, and devils would be subject to them.[Joh.14:12] They would have power over evil spirits.[Luk.9:1]

That does not mean that believers can impose salvation and freedom in lives against their will. Salvation comes to people when they hear the Gospel, believe it, and embrace Christ as Lord. When that is done, Satan's dominion over them ends. Jesus becomes their Master. Devils that have ruled their lives must then release them and surrender their control. If they do not depart at once, believers can act in Christ's name and command them to leave. *In my name you shall cast out devils,* Jesus said.

Paul speaks of *the exceeding greatness of God's power for [and in] us who believe, according to His mighty power, which He wrought in Christ, when He raised Him from the dead.*[Eph.1:19-20]

Christian believers have no need to fear evil spirits because those spirits *have been put under Christ's feet* [Eph.1:22] and believers have authority over them wherever the Gospel is believed.

Ministering Amidst Real Demons

Throughout our ministry in nations abroad, we have contended against the *powers of darkness* in order to liberate Satan's captives, bringing people out of spiritual slavery into God's new lifestyle.

We have consistently believed that Christ is with us, that God's Holy Spirit is in us, and that evil spirits are subject to us. If they do not flee from people when we proclaim the Gospel, then we cast them out. But we never say or do anything to indicate that we consider them a force *on par* with the Holy Spirit at work within us.

When we walk out on a platform amidst an ocean of people who know nothing of Christ, we *fight the good fight of faith* to bring light to those in darkness. We do our utmost to *persuade* them about the death and resurrection of Christ, and about how these events affect them.

Then every individual in that multitude has the right to accept and believe the Gospel, to embrace Christ as Lord and to receive His miracle blessings, or each one has the right of choice to reject the Gospel and the Christ-Life.

Strongholds Of *Un*-Belief

Paul talks about *persuading people* concerning Christ.[2Co.5:11; Gal.1:10] James says, *Whoever converts a sinner from the error of his way saves a soul from death.*[Jam.5:20] It requires a fight of faith to *pull down the strongholds* [2Co.10:4] of heathen religions and to break the superstitious power-grip of *non*-Christian cultures and pagan customs that often prevail among people abroad.

316

The same fight between the Good News and *un*-belief exists in the modern world. Unbelief is the same in any culture. People of both developed and underdeveloped worlds have the same right of choice.

MY WIFE AND I have borne witness of Christ and of His Gospel before millions of people, face to face. Always, we are surrounded by a multitude interspersed with the blind and deaf, the crippled and lame, the lost and bewildered, the hopeless and despairing, and with agents of sorcery and witchcraft, thugs, refugees, and those tormented by evil spirits.

It was the same during Christ's ministry. *They brought unto Him all sick people that were taken with divers diseases and torments, and those which were possessed with devils, and those which were lunatic, and those that had the palsy....* Mat.4:24

Ministering to a multitude like that is engaging in true spiritual warfare. It is *wrestling against real principalities and powers*—not imaginary or fictitious or synthetic spirits that people sometimes imagine in the western world. Every witness of Christ wrestles against those same powers when sharing the facts of the Gospel with anyone who is *un*-converted.

✧ ✧ ✧

CHAPTER SIXTY-NINE

WHAT THE FIGHT OF FAITH IS

PART 6 (ISSUE NO. 1)

FAITH—Warfare Intelligence

HOW DO WE fight this *fight of faith,* this fight to believe the facts of the Gospel even when they appear to be *foolishness* 1Co.1:18 and when situations seems to contradict our witness? What do we do?

It is critically important that we know the nature, the strength and the tactics of our enemy. Any army commander in war knows that his victory depends on the intelligence provided him.

Essential to defeating the enemy in warfare is knowledge of the potential of the opposing army's government.

Christians acquiesce before Satan's lies and accusations because they do not know 1) about Satan's total defeat by Christ, 2) about their own deliverance from Satan's power and dominion, and 3) about the fact that they have been brought back into companionship and rapport with God where *they stand unblameable and unreproachable in His sight.*[Col.1:22] Satan has no grounds for accusing or intimidating such people, but he does it to those who are not informed. He is a deceiver.

The next chapter in this book exposes the sham and chicanery of evil spirits in their charade against Christians. They have no power over believers. They may threaten, accuse, bluff or pretend, but there is no substance to their lies.

Satan's Restricted Power-Zone

It is indispensable for believers to know of Satan's defeat — to know that he is a deceiver, a liar, a bluff, a peddler of non-truths, a farce and an empty noise — so far as believers are concerned. His power-and-authority-zone is outside the Body of Christ, out amidst the *non*-converted world. He has no authority among Christians. For them, he is a defeated foe unless, of course, they choose to concede significance to him.

SO LET US LOOK at the truth about our defeated enemy. This brings us to the second essential issue about spiritual warfare that will elucidate and enrich the Christian believer's perspective of prayer and intercession. *What the Fight of faith is AGAINST.*

Chapter Seventy

What The Fight Of Faith Is Against

Part 1 (Issue No. 11)

The "Wiles" Of The Devil

PAUL SAID THAT our purpose in *fighting the faith fight* is to be able to *stand against the wiles of the devil.*[Eph.6:11] Never forget that our fight of faith is against "wiles" — not facts, but lies; not truth, but fraud; not reality, but delusion.

Believing Christians are not impressed by Satan's spurious threats. When they hear him bluff and intimidate, they systematically *cast down imaginations, and every thought that exalts itself against the knowledge of God.*[2Co.10:5] They renounce and reject whatever challenges biblical intelligence about Satan's defeat and about their own righteous standing in God's sight.

When Satan's emissaries suggest thoughts or when situations are confronted that are contrary to Gospel fact and redemptive truth, Christian believers realign their thoughts, vocabulary and actions with God's Word. That is what *fighting the good fight of faith* is all about.

Remember: Our faith is against "wiles" — fraudulence and cunning craftiness — not reality. We are believing God's Word in the face of forgery and deception by the enemy who is a liar and a deceiver.

If a Christian can be intimidated, frightened or manipulated by the devil's masquerading maneuvers and deception, he or she is believing Satan's lies instead of what God says. That is what Adam and Eve did in the Garden of Eden and, as a result, forfeited the blessed lifestyle that God planned for them.

Tricks And Traps Of The Traitor

When Paul referred to Satan's strategy, He talked of the *subtlety of the serpent (Satan),*[2Co.11:3] of his *craftiness,*[1Co.3:19] of how people can be *beguiled,*[Col.2:18] of how Satan *deceives the hearts of simple people.*[Rom.16:18] He warned the Ephesians of Satan's *cunning craftiness by which he deceives.*[Eph.4:14]

The *fight of faith* is to stand against the devil's *wiles* — not facts, but fraud. *Today's English Version* of the Bible says, *Stand up against the devil's evil tricks.* The *Living Bible* calls it, *strategies and tricks of Satan.* The *New International Version* translates it, *the devil's schemes. Phillips Modern English* translation uses the term, *the devil's craftiness.* The *New English Bible* is translated, *the devices of the devil.*

Believers in conflict with Satan are not confronting fact, but fraud. Satan's pretense is a charade.

Paul reminded believers that *we are not ignorant of Satan's devices,* and therefore, *he shall not get the advantage of us.*[2Co.2:11]

WHAT IS THE REAL meaning of these *wiles* and *devices* of Satan?

CHAPTER SEVENTY-ONE

WHAT THE FIGHT OF FAITH IS AGAINST

PART 2   (ISSUE No. 11)

Wiles And *Devices* Defined

THE MOST RESPECTED set of volumes for understanding New Testament vocabulary, acclaimed by Protestants, Catholics and Hebrew Rabbis alike, is *Kittel's Theological Dictionary of the New Testament*. It defines the words, *wiles* and *devices* thus:

Sensual and mental impressions. Philosophical perceptions. Purely mental activity having to do with emotional life and disposition. Sensual awareness, all in the mental sphere, as mental visions, sensations, modes of thought, mysticism. Echoes of religious mystery. Philosophical reflections. Corrupt or irrational human thoughts *of persons lacking in understanding.* Adverse religious judgments *by those deficient in an understanding of salvation.* Foolishness or folly in the sense of *insipientia* and also of *dementia.* [And much more.]

Satan's fraudulent duplicity and craftiness against Christians is a grand charade, a phony display of *non*-fact. Satan's trickery works only on those who attribute reality and substance to his *wiles.*

Satan's Only Power Over *Believers* Is What They *Concede* To Him

Satan's power is only authentic in the *non*-converted world, not in the lives of God's children. Believers have been rescued and *delivered out of the power of darkness, and translated into the kingdom of God's dear Son.*[Col.1:13] How could Satan's *wiles* (*un*-truths) affect those who are redeemed — unless they chose to believe his quackery?

A great degree of incapacitating superstition has historically manifested itself, in various forms, among church people.

Jesus said, *The devil has been a murderer from the beginning, and abides not in the truth, because there is no truth in him. When he speaks a lie, he speaks of his own: for he is a liar, and the father of it.*[Joh.8:44] That is very strong language! I cannot imagine how our Lord could have made it more clear that Satan is a farce who has no authority in our lives.

Satan The *Deluder* A *Liar* From The Beginning

To *fight the fight of faith* and *stand against the wiles of the devil* means to believe what God says instead of what Satan lies about. *There is no truth in him,*[Joh.8:44] Jesus said. Nothing that he says is authentic. His threats are empty — that is, for believers.

The only knowledge about Satan that the Christian should embrace is that he is an eternally defeated foe, stripped of all legal authority and power by Jesus Christ.

Satan's Rule Is Only Authentic In The *Non*-Converted World

Out in the *non*-believing world, Satan has authority to manipulate the *un*-converted. Why? Because the original sin of Adam and Eve gave him lordship and supremacy over every person who does not embrace the *redemptive* work of Jesus Christ.

326

Among Christian believers, Satan cannot suc-ceed because they know truth.[Joh.8:32] They do not believe lies. Jesus is *The Way* for them.[Joh.14:6] They are the *sheep of His flock.*[Joh.10:14] *A stranger they will not follow* [Joh.10:5] nor will they be moved or de-ceived or tricked by Satan's manipulation.

CHAPTER SEVENTY-TWO

WHAT THE FIGHT OF FAITH IS AGAINST

PART 3 (ISSUE No. 11)

Faith Against *Fraud*

THIS CHAPTER CONCERNS the Christian posture of standing against the *wiles of the devil*. We *fight the fight of faith* believing what God says instead of what Satan lies about.

We do as Solomon admonished: *We **attend** to [fix our mind on] God's words; we incline our **ears** to His sayings. We do not let them depart from our **eyes**; we keep them in the midst of our **heart**. For we know that they are **life** to us who find them, and **health** to all our flesh.*[Pro.4:20-22]

A Charade—An Illusion

John called our enemy *that old serpent, called the Devil, and Satan, which deceives the whole world.*[Rev.12:9] Note that he can only *deceive*. His works are a charade, an illusion.

No wonder John wrote with such joy when he said, *I heard a loud voice in heaven saying, Now is come salvation, and strength, and the kingdom of our God, and the power of His Christ: for the **accuser** of our brothers and sisters is cast down, which **accused** them before our God day and night.*[Rev.12:10] Satan constantly lies *to* us, and *about* us. He is a fraud, an accuser, a maligner.

Response To Deception

John said that *he heard a loud voice in heaven saying...they overcame the enemy by the blood of the Lamb, and by the Word of their testimony.*[Rev.12:10-11]

Christians resolve to see, to think, to believe and to speak only what their Lord has said in His Word. They are not influenced or intimidated by the liar's charade of crafty deception.

Standard Of God's Word

Job said, *My lips shall not speak wickedness, nor my tongue utter deceit.*[Job.27:4] He resolved never to contradict what he believed was God's goodness. He determined that he would never forsake his *integrity before God.*[Job 2:3]

David said, *By your words, Lord, I have kept me from the paths of the destroyer.*[Psa.17:4]

The believer's *fight of faith* is not against valid satanic authority and power. Satan has none, particularly in relation to those who are committed to Christ. The only power that he has or can exercise in the lives of Christ's followers is the power that they willingly concede to him.

The *serpent* [Gen.3:1] had no authority in the Garden of Eden. The Lord told Adam to *dress the garden and keep it.*[Gen.2:15] Obviously, Adam did not *keep* the garden, otherwise the serpent would not have been able to enter and plot his inducement to contravene God's plan.

Historic Human Tragedy
And Consequent Enslavement

God said, *Of the tree of the knowledge of good and evil, you shall not eat it: for in the day that you eat it you shall surely die.*[Gen.2:17]

But the serpent said, *You shall NOT surely die.*
^{Gen.3:4} The tragedy was that Adam and Eve believed the serpent's lie instead of God's Word.

They violated God's trust and acquiesced to Satan's deception. That was sin. It is still sin.

CHAPTER SEVENTY-THREE

WHAT THE
FIGHT OF FAITH IS
AGAINST

PART 4 (ISSUE No. 11)

Believers Not Bedazzled

WE FIGHT THE *fight of faith* in order to be able to *stand against the wiles of the devil,* that is against his lies and duplicity.

The Bible contains a litany of manifestations of Satan's deceitful wiles, such as:

Hidden things of dishonesty, craftiness and deceit.[2Co.4:2] *Sleight [fraud] of men and women [cf. Greek: Card-playing] and cunning craftiness.*[Eph.4:14] *Vanity of mind, understanding darkened, alienated from the life of God through ignorance, blindness of the heart.*[Eph.4:18] *Beguiled through subtilty; minds corrupted.*[2Co.11:3] *Speeches to deceive the hearts of the simple.*[Rom.16:18] *Imagined devices. Deceit, fraud, mischief, vanity, lurking places, murder of the innocent, as a lion crouches.*[Psa.10:2-10]

Mystery of iniquity, wicked revealed, consumed by the spirit of his mouth, the working of Satan, deceivableness, strong delusion that causes people to believe a lie; damned by not believing the truth.[2Th.2:7-12] *Shaken in mind, troubled, deceived.*[2Th.2:2-4] *Vanity of mind, blindness of heart.*[Eph.4:17-18] *Pernicious ways.*[2Pe.2:2]

Believers are to stand against these *wiles* and *devices* of Satan remembering that they are not facts, not realities, not substance. The Greek meanings include cunning arts, deceit, craft, trickery, error and being led astray from the right way by fraudulent means. Jesus said, *There is no truth in him.*[Joh.8:44]

CHAPTER SEVENTY-FOUR

WHAT THE FIGHT OF FAITH IS AGAINST

PART 5   (ISSUE NO. 11)

Security Or Vulnerability

A CHRISTIAN'S MINISTRY is to witness of Christ, to make known His truth. Christians are redeemed,[1Pe.1:18; Rev.5:9] free, and saved; restored to God;[2Co.5:19 LB] and delivered out of darkness.[Rom.7:6; Col.1:13]

The *non*-converted world is adrift, *without hope and without God.*[Eph.2:12] They are steeped in Satan's slavery and deception,[Rom.1:21-32] vulnerable to his *signs and lying wonders.*[2Th.2:9] They can only be delivered from Satan's rulership if we tell them about Christ and influence them to embrace Him as *The Way, the Truth and the Life.*[Joh.14:6]

So we *fight the good fight of faith*[1Ti.6:12] *standing against the wiles of the devil, wrestling against rulers of darkness in high places.* [Eph.6:11-12] We fight to rescue people from the destroyer. We need *the whole armor of God.* [Eph.6:11]

Equipment For *VICTORY*

Paul said, *The weapons of our warfare are not carnal, but mighty through God to the pulling down of strong holds; Casting down imaginations, and every high thing that exalts itself against the knowledge of God, and bringing into captivity every thought to the obedience of Christ.*[2Co.10:4-5]

IN THE NEXT CHAPTERS, we shall focus on the third vital issue that concerns spiritual warfare: What the armor of God *IS* and the significance of each element of the armor.

Once the believer has fitted himself or herself with these unbeatable elements of armor, Satan, with all of his craftiness, is no match.

CHAPTER SEVENTY-FIVE

WHAT <u>IS</u> THE ARMOR OF GOD

PART 1   (ISSUE No. III)

—TRUTH —

PAUL SAID, *Have the belt of truth buckled around your waist.*[Eph.6:14 NIV] When you know truth, you do not believe lies. Jesus is *the truth.*[Joh.14:6] Truth is not lies. John said, *No lie is of the truth.*[1Jo.2:21] Truth is liberating.[Joh.8:32] Truth is enlightenment.[Eph.1:18] Truth cannot be deceptive.

Paul said, *We gave no place [to Satan's messengers], no, not for an hour; that the **truth** of the Gospel might continue.*[Gal.2:5]

Paul said, *The Gospel of our salvation is the word of **truth**, and after that we believed, we were sealed with the Holy Spirit of promise.*[Eph.1:13]

Later he said, *When we receive the Word of God, which is **truth**, it effectually works in us who believe.*[1Th.2:13]

Truth That Saves

Paul said that the reason for sharing the Gospel with the *non*-converted is because *God yearns for all people to be saved, and to come to the knowledge of **truth**.*[1Ti.2:4]

Truth is our strength, our defense. Our loins are girded with truth concerning Jesus Christ and what He accomplished for us. We never tremble before the wiles or devices of the devil because we know the truth about his defeat, about his authority having been annulled. We are not intimidated or disquieted by the deceiver's lies or threats. Our faith is unshakable because of our knowledge of redemptive truth.

Chapter Seventy-Six

What IS The ARMOR Of God

Part 2 (Issue No. III)

- RIGHTEOUSNESS -

PUT ON THE *breastplate of* RIGHTEOUSNESS. Eph.6:14 Now that our sins have been laid on Christ and He has endured the judgment that we deserved, *His righteousness has been imputed to us,* Rom.4:22,24 credited to our account. Rom. 4:5; 5:17-18

The devil endeavors to make us question our salvation, our security, our identity, our standing before God in righteousness, our oneness with our Lord. We can repudiate Satan's demeaning suggestions because *we know in whom we have believed.*[2Ti.1:12] *We know that we have passed from death unto life.*[1Jo.3:14]

We can stand in the midst of any temptation or trial or battle with unshakable faith because we are believers in the unchangeable Christ. We wear the *breastplate of His righteousness.* That is how we stand against the *wiles of the devil.*

We know that Christ's righteousness is ours.[1Co.1:30] Satan cannot touch us.[1Jo.5:18] He only bluffs. Our righteousness is greater and more secure than any stronghold of the devil in high places.

Our old nature died with Christ and was buried with Him; then we came up out of death with Him into a new Life...He gave us a share in the very Life of Christ...and blotted out all charges proved against us...In this way **God took away Satan's power to accuse us of sin***, and He openly displayed to the whole world Christ's triumph at the Cross where our sins were all taken away.*[Col.2:12-15 LB]

The Armor Of Righteousness

That is why *there is therefore now no condemnation to them that are in Christ Jesus.*[Rom.8:1]

We march forward *by the Word of truth, by the power of God, by the armor of righteousness on the right hand and on the left.*[2Co.6:7]

No wonder we are winners! The victory that the Captain of our Salvation [Heb.2:10] bought and paid for by laying down His life for us is our victory. He conquered our enemy by coming back from the dead. With this knowledge, none of the phony chicanery of the devil can destabilize or exacerbate us. *We are not ignorant of his devices.*[2Co.2:11] We wear the *breastplate of Christ's righteousness.* We are armed against the accusations of the enemy.

The armor of God enables us to *stand against the wiles [the deceitfulness, fakery, empty threats, fraudulence, lying wonders] of the devil.*[Eph.6:11]

How could any believer imagine that devils could wield power in their lives? Never! *Christ is our Life.*[Col.3:4] *Christ is made unto us righteousness.*[1Co.1:30] Righteousness is our *breastplate.*[Eph.6:14] We are right with God.

CHAPTER SEVENTY-SEVEN

WHAT IS THE ARMOR OF GOD

PART 3   (ISSUE No. III)

– PEACE –

HAVE *YOUR FEET* shod with the preparation of *the Gospel of peace.*[Eph.6:15] The *New English Bible* says it like this: *Let the shoes on your feet be the Gospel of peace, to give you firm footing.*

Adam Clarke's remarkable commentary dated 1831 says: The metal *greaves* [1Sa.17:6] "to protect the soldier's feet were deemed essential in ancient armor: if the feet or legs were wounded, a soldier could neither stand to resist his foe, pursue him if vanquished, nor flee from him, should he have the worst of the fight."

The Beautiful Feet Of Christ's Messengers

Paul speaks of the Gospel messenger's feet, quoting Isaiah: *How beautiful upon the mountains are the feet of those who bring good tidings, who publish peace; who bring good tidings of good, who publish salvation; who says to Zion, your God reigns!*[Isa.52:7]

Before exiting Egypt, the Israelites were commanded to eat the Passover with their *feet shod,* [Exo.12:11] to show that they were prepared for their journey. Jesus told His disciples to be *shod with sandals,*[Mar.6:9] ready to go and publish the Gospel *into all the world and to every creature.*[Mar.16:15]

Christian believers are like marching soldiers sharing the Gospel of peace with a despairing world. They need their feet well shod, protected against gall-traps and sharp sticks in their pathway, concealed there by enemy agents. If they fell upon them, they would be wounded and perhaps disabled for battle.

Shod For The Mission

Paul says, *Have your feet shod with the preparation of the Gospel of peace.* The word translated *preparation* is understood to mean that the believer is ready to witness for Christ. It means *firmness and readiness in the one who believes the Gospel enough to tell it to others.*

Paul emphasized that the armor of believers must include strong, protected feet because their mandate is to go out, as Jesus said, *into the highways and hedges, compelling them [i.e., the unconverted] to come in.*[Luk.14:23]

The historian, Josephus, tells us that the soldiers under Alexander the Great and Julius Caesar were shod with strong army boots *[caligae]* "thickly studded with sharp nails" [(Josephus)] to ensure toughness and a good grip. Triumph in battle depended on soldiers being well shod for long-distant marches over rough and treacherous terrain.

Remember, we are talking about *putting on the whole armor of God, to stand against the wiles [the lies, the deceit, the forgery] of the devil.*

Peace Instead Of Perversion

This chapter concerns *the Gospel of Peace!* Believers can only have peace when they know the truth about redemption. Only then can they stand against the lying accusations of Satan.

With their feet planted on the solid rock of faith in Christ, Christian believers know that they are *reconciled to God* [2Co.5:18] and that *the Word of reconciliation has been committed unto them.*[2Co.5:18-19]

Their *feet are shod with the Gospel of peace.* They are right with God and they stand before Him without the consciousness of sin, fear, guilt or inferiority.[Col.1:22; 1Th.3:13] With peace, believers are not destabilized or discomfited by the incriminating harassment of the devil.

Peace Through Reconciliation

Peace is knowing that every sin is paid for, that the judgment of one's sin has already been suffered by Christ on the Cross, and that *there is therefore now no condemnation to them who are in Christ Jesus.*[Rom.8:1]

Peace is knowing that Christ, *the Captain of our Salvation, has rescued us out of the darkness and gloom of Satan's kingdom and brought us into the kingdom of God's dear Son, who bought our freedom with His blood and forgave us all our sins.*[Col.1:13-14 LB]

Peace is knowing that *Christ's death on the Cross has made peace with God for all of us, by His blood, including you and I who were far away from Him...yet now He has brought us back into the pres-*

ence of God as His friends through Christ's death on the Cross, and we are standing there with nothing left against us...the only condition being that we fully believe the Truth...convinced of the Good News that Jesus died for us, and never shifting from trusting Him to save us. This is the wonderful news that...is spreading all over the world. And we have the joy of telling it to others. Col.1:20-23 LB

Never shifting from trusting Him. That is the secret. That is the Gospel of peace.

Prepared To Pursue Peace

To carry that message of peace amidst *evil principalities and rulers of darkness and to stand against the wiles of the devil,* believers must have their feet well shod for their march. They must be protected against the deceitful traps and sharp accusations or disabling and lying indictments of the devil that would wound or intimidate or weaken their progress in witnessing.

CHAPTER SEVENTY-EIGHT

WHAT IS THE ARMOR OF GOD

PART 4 (ISSUE No. III)

– FAITH –

ABOVE ALL, TAKE the shield of FAITH, with which you shall be able to quench all the fiery darts of the wicked. Eph.6:16

Satan is the *accuser*. Rev.12:10 His demeaning *darts* of recrimination, disparagement and slander can inflict stinging and infectious wounds that would weaken or destroy confidence if it were not for well-grounded *faith* in what Christ accomplished on behalf of believers.

The Preeminent Element

Paul urged: ***above all,*** *take the shield of* ***faith.*** Most vital for standing against the *wiles of the devil* is believing God's Word. When we choose God's Word over Satan's lies, we repulse the shrewd suggestions and demeaning accusations of the devil because *we are not ignorant of his devices.* [2Co.2:11]

Without faith it is impossible to please God: for who-ever comes to Him must believe that He is, and that He is a rewarder of them that diligently seek Him. [Heb.11:6]

Yes, *Above all...take the shield of faith!*

Faith Against Fables

Satan mesmerizes the *un*-believing world with his fallacious fabrications. The believer who is grounded in God's Word is not swayed by appearances or illusions that repudiate what the Lord has said. *Faith* is *believing the Word of God in the face of all contradictions.*

Jesus said, *Have faith in God.* [Mar.11:22] He said, *If you have faith as a grain of mustard seed, you shall say to this mountain, Remove from here to that place; and it shall remove; and nothing shall be impossible for you.* Mat.17:20

The prophet Habakkuk said, *The just shall live by faith.* Hab.2:4 Paul repeated those words twice, Rom.1:17; Gal.3:11 and the writer of Hebrews also stated them. Heb.10:38

Jesus — Faith-Builder

Jesus constantly taught faith. He commended those who expressed faith, such as the centurion, Mat. 8:10; Luk.7:9 the woman of Canaan, Mat.15:28 and the woman with the issue of blood. Mar.5:25; Luk.8:48 He rewarded those with faith like the man with palsy, Mat.9:2; Mar.2:5; Luk.5:20 the woman in need, Mat.9:22; Luk.8:48 the two blind men, Mat.9:29 and blind Bartimaeus. Mar.10:52 He prayed for Peter that his *faith would not fail.* Luk.22:32

Paul urged, *Above all take the shield of faith.*

Faith in what? Faith in what God has said. *Faith comes by hearing the Word of God.* Rom.10:17 If Christians do not believe what the Bible says about their relationship with Him and about what Christ accomplished on their behalf, then they are vulnerable to the accusations of the Wicked One.

Knowledge — Not Ignorance

But Christians are **believers**. They *walk by faith and not by sight.* 2Co.5:7 They *are not ignorant of Sa-*

tan's devices.[2Co.2:11] They do not fall for his *lying wonders*.[2Th.2:9] They are like Abraham, *fully persuaded that, what God promised, he is able also to perform*.[Rom.4:21] Paul said, *we know whom we have believed, and are persuaded that He is able to keep that which we have committed unto Him*.[2Ti.1:12]

We know that our enemy is defeated. Our faith enables us to *quench all the fiery darts of the wicked*.[Eph.6:16] We are unmoved by Satan's demagoguery and threatening masquerades of perfidious tactics to demean, demoralize, deprecate and disparage us. He is a *liar* and *no truth is in him*. We know that, and we *quench his fiery darts*.

Chapter Seventy-Nine

What IS The ARMOR Of God

Part 5   (Issue No. 111)

- SALVATION -

*T*AKE THE HELMET of SALVATION.^{Eph.6:17} Many Christians lack assurance about their salvation. At the least accusation by Satan, they become insecure, wondering whether or not they are right with God.

Paul instructs us never to question our salvation. He said that *through the death of Christ on the Cross, He brought us back to God as His friends [back into the presence of God] standing there before Him with nothing left against us...convinced of the Good News that Jesus died for us, and never shifting from trusting Him....* Col.1:21-23 LB

Unblameable—Unreproveable

To underscore our standing with God, Paul said that Christ, *in the body of His flesh through death, presented us holy and unblameable and unreproveable in His sight.* Col.1:22

Paul said that the Lord wants to *establish our hearts unblameable in holiness before God, our Father.* 1Th.3:13

Spiritual insecurity and trepidation before God is a centuries-old dilemma. Some church denominations still teach that one cannot be certain of his or her salvation; that one can only hope that, at the end, one will be saved.

John said, *We **know** that we have passed from death unto life.* 1Jo.3:14 If we do not know that, we cannot *stand against the wiles [deceitfulness and accusing maneuvers] of the devil.* Eph.6:11

We are talking about *wrestling against principalities, rulers of the darkness, and spiritual wickedness in high places.* Eph.6:12 These powers are not within the

Church of believers. The powers that we *wrestle against* are in the *un*-converted world where we are commissioned to carry the Gospel as Christ's witnesses.[Acs.1:8; 5:32]

Witnessing Among The *Non*-Converted

Giving witness of the Gospel of Christ, we look into the faces of *un*-converted people and tell them that Christ has borne their sins, that He loves them, and that their salvation has been paid in full. We say that boldly with faith because, as Paul said, *We believe the truth...we are convinced of the Good News that Jesus died for us, and we never shift from trusting Him.*[Col.1:21-23 LB]

If we are not confident of our own salvation, we will live in spiritual indecision and vacillation, susceptible to intimidation by Satan's wiles. In such a state we can never be convincing in our witness of Christ to others.

To be Christ's witness, sharing His Good News with the *un*-converted out where Satan's principalities dominate as rulers of darkness, we must wear *the helmet of salvation.*[Eph.6:17]

Convinced Of Christ's Righteousness

In other words, we must be convinced of our own salvation. We must be at peace in our own hearts. We must trust what Christ has done for us. We must believe that we stand before God

holy, unblameable and unreproveable in His sight.
Col.1:22

To wear the *helmet of salvation* means that we have confidence in our own right standing before God. Since we have *heard Christ's Word, and have believed on God who sent Him, we have everlasting Life, and shall not come into condemnation; but we are passed from death unto life.*Joh.5:24 We believe that. We are confident.

*Beloved, if our heart does not condemn us, then we have confidence toward God.*1Jo.3:21 *So now, abide in Him; that...you may have confidence, and not be ashamed before Him....*1Jo.2:28

Knowing The Scriptures
Believing The Gospel

*The Lord is my light and my salvation; whom shall I fear? the Lord is the strength of my life; of whom shall I be afraid?*Psa.27:1

*Behold, God is my salvation; I will trust, and not be afraid: for the Lord Jehovah is my strength and my song; He also is become my salvation.*Isa.12:2

*Being justified by faith, we have peace with God through our Lord Jesus Christ: By whom also we have access by faith into this grace wherein we stand, and rejoice in hope of the glory of God.*Rom.5:1-2

Saved By Grace Through Faith

*For by grace are we saved through faith; and that not of ourselves: it is the gift of God: Not of works, lest anyone should boast. For we are His workmanship, created in Christ Jesus.*Eph.2:8-10

And [we are] found in Him, not having our own righteousness,...but that which is through the faith of Christ, the righteousness which is of God by faith:
Phi.3:9

*Jesus said, whoever hears my Word, and believes on Him who sent me, has everlasting Life, and shall not come into condemnation; but is passed from death unto Life.*Joh.5:24

No More Condemnation

There is therefore now no condemnation to them who are in Christ Jesus, who walk not after the flesh, but after the Spirit. For the law of the Spirit of Life in Christ Jesus has made me free from the law of sin and death.
Rom.8:1-2

*Who is he that condemns us? It is Christ who died, yes rather, who is risen again, who is at the right hand of God, who makes intercession for us. Who can separate us from the love of Christ?*Rom.8:34-35

Redemption Through Christ's Blood

*For Christ was slain, and has redeemed us to God by His blood out of every kindred, and tongue, and people, and nation.*Rev.5:9

*He loved us, and washed us from our sins in His own blood.*Rev.1:5

The Lord Jesus said, *This is my blood of the new testament, which is shed for many for the remission of sins.* Mat.26:28

*Whoever believes in Him should not perish, but have eternal life.*Joh.3:15 *And whoever shall call on the name of the Lord shall be saved.*Acs.2:21

Our Faithful Savior

John said, *If we confess our sins, He is faithful and just to forgive us our sins, and to cleanse us from all unrighteousness.*1Jo.1:9

He reminds us that *Jesus did many other signs in the presence of His disciples, which are not written in this book: But these are written, that you might believe that Jesus is the Christ, the Son of God; and that believing you may have life through His name.*Joh.20:30-31

Paul's Witness In A Superstitious City

Paul understood what this *fight of faith* is. He had stood in the vast amphitheater at Athens and witnessed for Christ before a people who were *too superstitious,*[Acs.17:22] dominated by *principalities, powers, rulers of darkness and spiritual wickedness in high places.*

He told the Athenians, *The Lord of heaven and earth does not dwell in temples made with hands; neither is worshipped with men's hands...because He gives to all life and breath,...*and he urged them to *seek the Lord...and find Him...because in Him we live and move and have our being,...and we are His offspring, so we ought not to think that the Godhead is like gold, or silver, or stone, graven by art and man's device.* Then he witnessed in that pagan amphitheater that God has *raised Jesus from the dead.*
Acs.17:24-31

In such an ambiance, Paul was *fighting the fight of faith* amidst *principalities, powers, and spiritual wickedness in high places.*

These powers and rulers are not inside the Church, the Body of Christ. They are not among Christian believers. They are outside the Church in the *un*-converted world of the *un*-saved who know nothing of the redemptive work of Jesus Christ.

Paul yearned for followers of Christ to be armed for their ministry of witnessing in the *non*-converted world so that they could go amidst perverse darkness and spiritual wickedness and be able to *stand against the wiles of the devil.*

356

WHAT IS THE ARMOR OF GOD

Ministry Of Reconciliation

Paul had the picture in clear focus. To him it was vital that Christians understand how *God has reconciled us to Himself by Jesus Christ.*[2Co.5:18] That is our salvation. That is accomplished. We have peace. We believe that Christ did *enough* to save us. We trust in *His* merits for our salvation — not in *ours*.

Then, speaking of our reconciliation, Paul continues to the next step, which is our ministry. He says: *and God has given to **us** the ministry of reconciliation.*[2Co.5:18-19]

Reconciling *Un*-believers To God

The believer's function in God's family is to be Christ's witness and to reconcile people to God. That ministry is now *entrusted into our hands.*
[2Co.5:19; 1Th.2:4; 1Ti.1:11;]

Paul knew this so he urged us: "Be sure that you wear the *helmet of salvation.*" In other words, be sure that you are confident of your own standing before God. If not, Satan will accuse you, lie to you, bluff you, confuse you, deceive you and defeat you by his cunning *devices* and *wiles*.

CHAPTER EIGHTY

WHAT IS THE ARMOR OF GOD

PART 6   (ISSUE No. 111)

– THE WORD –

*T*AKE THE SWORD *of the Spirit, which is the* WORD *of God.*Eph.6:17 Paul knew that it is essential for the Christian to know God's redemptive plan, to know what salvation means and to know the Word of God.

Believers must know four biblical truths that constitute the Gospel.
1. God's creation
2. Satan's deception
3. Christ's substitution
4. Our restoration

Believers must know that
a. Our redemption is a fact;
b. Satan is defeated;
c. Christ's victory is our victory;
d. His righteousness is ours;
e. *As He is, so are we in this world.* [1Jo.4:17; Joh.17:18; 20:21]

Know *Yourself* In The Scriptures

Believers must know **themselves** in the Bible. Jesus Christ knew who He was. *And beginning at Moses and all the prophets, he expounded in all the scriptures the things **concerning Himself**.* [Luk.24:27] Jesus could point to the ancient Scriptures of the Hebrew prophets and identify Himself throughout the sacred text.

The Jews *sought to kill Jesus, because...He said that God was His Father, making Himself equal with God.* [Joh.5:18] He told them, *Search the scriptures; for...they testify **of me**.* [v.39]

Jesus Himself quoted the ancient Hebrew prophecies that related to Himself. [Mat.26:56; Luk.21:22; 24:44; Joh.15:25; 17:12] His faith in His relationship with

His Father was based on His knowledge of the Scriptures.

Christ Came To
Show Us—*US*

Regarding His faith, Jesus Christ believed the same Scriptures that we are to believe. They spoke about *Him*. They speak about *us*. His purpose in coming to our level was to show us — *US*; to show us that if we follow Him and believe on Him, we can share the same rapport and relationship with the Father that He has.[Joh.14:12; 17:18,21-23]

Numerous prophecies about Jesus are quoted in the Gospels.[Mat.1:22; 2:15,23; 4:14; 8:17; 12:17; 13:35; 21:4; 27:35; Joh.12:38; 19:24] Jesus knew Himself in the Scriptures.

Many prophecies about the coming Messiah are recorded in the Old Testament. Christ knew them. They were the source of His faith. That was why He could confront demons and they would flee before Him, obeying His commands. *They* knew that *He* knew who He was in the Scriptures.

Christ's faith was based on what His Father had spoken through the Prophets. Our faith is founded on the Scriptures that speak about *us*.

Discovering *Ourselves* In God's Word

You and I must know who we are in the Bible. Knowledge of truth is the only sure foundation for faith. (Remember, we are talking about Paul's counsel for us to *fight the fight of faith, to stand against Satan's wiles and devices*.)

We must, as John said, **know** *that we are passed from death unto life.*[1Jo.3:14] No lying suggestion or deceptive illusion that Satan conjures up can move us, intimidate us, or cause us to *shift from trusting Christ* [Col.1:23 LB] when we know ourselves in the Scriptures.

Aware Of The Scriptures

Paul knew who he was in Christ. He testified: *God, who separated me from my mother's womb, called me by his grace, to reveal his Son in me, that I might preach Him among the heathen.*[Gal.1:15-16]

Paul witnessed that the Lord said to him: *Rise, and stand on your feet: for I have appeared to you...to make you a minister and a witness both of these things which you have seen, and of those things in which I will appear to you.*[Acs.26:16]

Paul knew the Scriptures about himself. During his early years of religious fanaticism, He had been blinded by prejudice against Christ, but when the Lord appeared to him *as he journeyed and came near Damascus, and the light from heaven shined round about him, he fell to the earth,*[Acs.9:3-4] and his life was transformed.

Straightway, Paul preached Christ in the synagogues, that He is the Son of God…confounding the Jews,…proving that this Jesus is the Christ.[Acs.9:20,22] He *reasoned with people **out of the Scriptures**.*[Acs.17:2] He *mightily convinced the Jews publicly, showing **by the Scriptures** that Jesus was Christ.*[Acs.18:28]

*Paul preached that which he also received, how that Christ died for our sins **according to the scriptures**; And that He was buried, and that He rose again the third day **according to the Scriptures**.*[1Co.15:3-4]

During Paul's final months, prior to his martyrdom at Rome, *many came to his lodging; to whom he expounded and testified the kingdom of God, persuading them concerning Jesus, from both the **Law of Moses and the Prophets**, from morning till evening.*[Acs.28:23] Paul knew the Scriptures. He knew himself in the Scriptures.

To *stand against the wiles of the devil, we are to take the sword of the Spirit which is the Word of God.* Eph.6:17

What We *Know* By The Scriptures

By God's Word, we **know** *that we have passed from death unto Life.*[1Jo.3:14] Paul said, **Know** *the things that are freely given us of God.*[1Co.2:12]

By His Word, we *know the grace of our Lord Jesus Christ.*[2Co.8:9] We *know the love of Christ which passes human knowledge.*[Eph.3:19]

We *know Him and the power of His resurrection.*[Phi.3:10] *We know whom we have believed, and are persuaded that He is able to keep that which we have committed to Him against that day.*[2Ti.1:12]

By the Scriptures, we *know that we were not redeemed with silver and gold,...but with the precious blood of Christ, as of a lamb without blemish and without spot.*[1Pe.1:18-19]

John says, we *know that we know Jesus Christ.*[1Jo.2:3] *We know that we are in Him.*[v.5] *We know that Christ was manifested to take away our sins; and in Him is no sin.*[1Jo.3:5]

By the Word of God, we *know that we have passed from death unto Life.*[1Jo.3:14] *We know that we are of the truth.*[1Jo.3:19] *We know that He abides in us by the Spirit which He has given us.*[v.24] *We know that we have eternal Life.*[1Jo.5:13] *We know that we are of God.*[v.19]

Faith Is *KNOWING*

It is by knowing the Scriptures that our faith is unshakable before Satan's *cunning devices.* We can *stand against the wiles [deceitfulness] of the devil* because we are equipped with *the sword of the Spirit which is the Word of God.*

363

Knowing the facts of the Gospel and knowing ourselves in the Scriptures, we are not suceptible to Satan's *wiles* and *devices* as we witness of Christ among the *un*-converted.

We *fight the fight of faith,...equipped with the sword of the Spirit which is the Word of God.*

CHAPTER EIGHTY-ONE

WHAT IS THE ARMOR OF GOD

PART 7   (ISSUE No. III)

– PRAYER –

*P*RAYING ALWAYS...*watching with all persever-ance.*[Eph.6:18] To minister or to witness of Christ effectively in the *non*-converted world where *principalities* and *spiritual wickedness* reign, we must always do it prayerfully.

Many Christians miss the Bible focus of spiritual warfare. They often limit it to sanctuary prayer and intercession for delivering other Christians from evil spirits. Their imaginations are introverted and self-centered by unbalanced and *non*-redemptive teaching.

Confusion About Christian Ministry

To relate Paul's counsel about spiritual warfare to ministry among Christians would be like relating Christ's Great Commission to a ministry *of* believers *for* believers.

For example, Jesus never conceived of His followers assembling themselves together and casting evil spirits out of each other.[Mar.16:17] His statement, *they shall cast out devils*, was a sign that would follow believers who would preach or teach the Gospel in *all the world*.[Mar.16:15] If they met demon-possessed people such as the man of Gadara [Luk.8:27-33] or the Syrophenician girl,[Mar.7:24-29] Jesus assured them that they could cast out the evil spirits. His words were not instructing Christians to cast out evil spirits from other Christians.

Poisonous Drinks

When Jesus told His followers, *If you drink any deadly thing, it will not hurt you*,[Mar.16:18] He did not conceive of believers being poisoned in their own meetings, assuring them that *it would not hurt them.*Mar.16:18 He was speaking to His followers about events that might occur as they went to the *non*-believing, *un*-converted world to share the Good News of Christ.

Snake Handlers

Certain cult leaders and their members practice handling venomous serpents during their "worship." They are introverted and self-centered in their "faith." Jesus never conceived of His followers bringing serpents into their meeting places, then handling them, being bitten by them, and proving their "spirituality" by His words, *They shall take up serpents.*Mar.16:18 This is egocentric, narcisistic and self-aggrandizing.

Visualizing Evil Spirits In Believers

It is equally vainglorious and self-indulgent for Christians to meet together and imagine that they are casting evil spirits out of each other. To do that is to denigrate the miracle of the new birth and the regenerating power of the Life of Jesus Christ that is received when He is embraced as Lord and Savior.

It is spiritually juvenile to consider Christ's commission concerning "casting out devils" as a function of "saints" ministering to "saints." His words were directed to His followers whom He was sending as His witnesses *into all the world.*^{Mar.16:15}

Casting Out Devils — In The World
Overcoming Devils — In The Church

Paul counselled the followers of Christ to put on *the whole armor of God, and fight the fight of faith* so that they could *stand against the wiles of the devil.*

The apostle was not counseling Christians to pray, intercede and struggle in "spiritual warfare" among themselves, imagining demons being exorcised from one another, or dispelling evil spirits from their homes or neighborhoods or businesses or places of worship or communities. That sort of thing is superstition, not spiritual warfare.

Such visualization misses the target and becomes the ritual of persons who have not matured in their faith, but who have remained self-centered *children* in their spiritual perspective.

To succeed in prayer, Christians are not to be *children in understanding; they are to be mature.*
1Co.14:20 NJK

368

Praying Always–For What?
The Key To Christian Ministry

Praying always, the apostle counseled. Praying for WHAT? Here is the key to Christian ministry as witnesses of Christ. Pray *that utterance may be given to us, that we may open our mouths boldly to make known the mystery of the Gospel.*Eph.6:19

The *fight of faith against principalities and powers* is the Christian's struggle to *make known the mystery of the Gospel* – out in the *un*-converted world where *rulers of darkness* reign, out where opposition is fierce, out where the believer's life may be jeopardized. Jesus said, *The field is the world.*Mat.13:38

Praying For *Utterance*
To Make Known The Gospel

During Paul's witnessing of Christ in Macedonia, the mob rose up and the magistrates *commanded to beat Paul and Silas and laid many stripes upon them, casting them into prison.*Acs.16:22-23 While in that area, Paul wrote to the believers at Thessalonica: *Pray for us, that the Word of the Lord may have free course...and that we may be delivered from unreasonable and wicked men.*2Th.3:1-2

That is an example of *fighting the fight of faith against principalities and rulers of darkness*. Paul *pulled down the strongholds* of Macedonia and as a result of his witnessing, strong churches were birthed.

Now you can understand why Paul urged that our armor include *praying always with all supplication and perseverance.* For what? That *utterance may be given to us to make known the mystery of the Gospel* — where? Inside the walls of places of worship? No! Outside those walls, out amidst *non*-believers. Paul said to pray that *the word of the Lord can have free course* — outside the fellowship of believers in the Body of Christ, out amidst *unreasonable and wicked people.*

Peter Urges Readiness

Peter urged believers to *be ready always to give an answer to everyone who asks you a reason for the hope that is in you.*[1Pe.3:15] That is our ministry — out where *non*-believers are asking, "Why do you believe this *foolishness* about Jesus dying for the sins of the world and being raised from the dead?"

We are Christ's witnesses. We must be convincing. We must be given *utterance.* We are making known the mystery of the Gospel. We are *fighting the fight of faith,* giving the message of Christ where we must *wrestle against evil powers,* out where *rulers of darkness* reign.

Concepts Incompatible
With *Redemptive* Truth

Christians who are narcissistic in their view of spiritual warfare miss the point, being influenced by voices that contradict redemptive truth and that assert concepts that are incompatible with Paul's revelation of the new creation in Christ.

I said earlier in this book that from Bible days until now, young believers have been confused and disquieted by the voices of those who lack knowledge about or demean what Christ accomplished in His death and resurrection.

Paul alerted Christians to *beware lest anyone spoil you through philosophy.*[Col.2:8] He spoke of those who are *proud and...destitute of the truth.*[1Ti.6:4-5] He said, *Vain talkers...would subvert whole houses...for filthy lucre's sake* [Tit.1:10-11] *and would make merchandise of people.*[2Pe.2:1-3]

It is vital that Christians be aware of their rights in Christ and that they be secure in their knowledge of salvation through faith in God's unchangeable Word so that they can stand against Satan's deceptions without wavering.

Prayer
Element Of God's Armor

Prayer is part of the believer's armor. Prayer that is not based on knowledge can be fanaticism.

Pagans pray and cry; they scream and pound their chests. They contend against evil spirits which they believe they must chase away by offering blood sacrifices, by lengthy incantations, by drums, dancing and noise, and by the intervention of mediating witchdoctors engaged to officiate at rituals.

The members of almost every religion that we have encountered in nearly eighty nations espouse certain strange concepts about demon spirits. They are preoccupied with the presence and power of evil spirits which they visualize as being destructive and that bring disasters, diseases and evil upon themselves and upon their communities.

Their biggest defense against these evil powers is to bring animals or fowls for a priest to sacrifice while they cry, yell, agonize, rebuke and contend with these demonic powers, voicing curses against them, interceding and exorcising them from their midst.

The *non*-converted world is full of such practices that express pagan faith in demons.

I am told that there are more witchdoctors in France than there are medical professionals. Witchcraft is inundating Great Britain and Europe. In those remarkable nations where faith in the Gospel has been attributed to medieval superstition for decades, those same cultured, educated, modern people have been turning *pell-mell* to witchcraft during this and recent decades.

The armor that Paul says for us to put on includes prayer and supplication. The armor element of *Prayer* must coincide with the other six elements: 1) Truth, 2) Righteousness, 3) Peace, 4) Faith, 5) Salvation, and 6) God's Word.

Fused with knowledge about these other elements, prayer becomes the vital intercourse between the believer and his or her Lord.

Our Futile Prayers Without Knowledge

From the time that Jesus appeared to me and we began this world ministry, each morning we were on our knees praying for at least two hours. Our ministry is founded on prayer and intercession. We believe in prayer. We pray.

But before we understood about redemption, we prayed for many hours in futility. Before we launched our first Healing Crusade in America, I went into the basement of our home where I prayed and fasted for three days (without a drop of water or a crumb of food). I was interceding for God to heal the sick *for us* when we laid our hands on them in our upcoming meetings.

After three days, I seemed to hear the echo of my voice. But it was in the form of a question. "Heal them—*for whom?*" I stammered, "Heal the sick *for us*, O Lord, when we lay our hands on them." And the voice came again: "*For whom?*"

I pondered: Two thousands years before we became interested in healing for sick people, God was so moved with compassion for those who suffer that He sent His Son who gave His back to the smiters who *ploughed his flesh like a farmer ploughs furrows in a field,*Psa.129:3 *and by those stripes we are healed.*Isa.53:5

There I was, fasting and praying for God to have enough interest in sick people to "heal them for us—*for us!*" —as though *He* was not as interested in them as we were. I was interceding and fasting, but I was ignoring redemptive truth.

That is an example of how people agonize in prayer about devils. We do not have to do that. Our part is to give the Gospel to our hurting world and to give it with faith. God will confirm it. Salvation is *His* idea. We do not have to agonize with Him to get Him interested in delivering people from Satan's captivity.

CHAPTER EIGHTY-TWO

YOUR VICTORY IS WON

THERE WILL BE NO more lost battles at your house—nor at ours! Devils may roar and threaten, but John said that when we are born of God in a new birth, *that wicked one touches us not.*[1Jo.5:18]

When Satan approaches us now, he has to deal with our Lord. Christ lives at our house. He said, *My Father and I will come to you and make our abode with you.*[Joh.14:23]

We are no longer losers in life's battles. *Thanks be to God, who gives us the victory through our Lord Jesus Christ.*[1Co.15:57]

The death of Christ signaled that all of our sins have been remitted and that Satan can no longer

condemn us. We are translated out of his dominion. Satan knows this and therefore, when we *re-*
sist the devil, he flees from us.[Jam.4:7]

If God be for us, who can be against us?[Rom.8:31] *Who*
shall lay anything to our charge as God's elect? It is
God who has [already] justified us.[v.33]

When God raised Jesus from the dead, He took
from Satan *the keys of hell and of death.*[Rev.1:18] His
triumph over Satan was our triumph. Now *be-*
cause He lives, we live also. [Joh.14:19]

Our adversary, is conquered. Sin and evil, disease and suffering, poverty and failure have been
defeated by Christ. He has become our Partner,
our Associate in life.

Overcomers In *Victory*

Now is come salvation, and strength, and the king-
dom of our God, and the power of Christ; for our ac-
cuser (Satan) is cast down, who accused us before God
day and night. And we overcome him by the blood of
the Lamb, and by the Word of our testimony.[Rev.12:10-11]

Now we are triumphant. Satan no longer defeats us because He *whose name is called The Word*
of God [Rev.19:13] *dwells in us* [Joh.14:17] *and we have re-*
demption through His blood.[Col.1:14]

Our Lord says, *all power [all authority] is given*
unto me in heaven and earth...and lo, I am with you
alway, even unto the end of the world.[Mat.28:18,20]

So we can say, *The life which we now live in the flesh, we live by the faith of the Son of God, who loved us, and gave Himself for us.*[Gal.2:20] *All things are ours ...and we are Christ's, and Christ is God's.*[1Co.3:21-23]

Christ came to give us abundant Life.[Joh.10:10] He fought our battles and won our victory. He abrogated our enemy's authority and now, we only think of Satan as a defeated foe. His power and jurisdiction over us are finished. We are delivered. We are saved. We are free. When Satan tries to touch us now, he touches God's property that is redeemed.[1Pe.1:18; Rev.5:9]

Provisions For *All*

The purpose of communicating the Gospel is to inform people of these provisions which are purchased for *every creature in all the world* [Mar.16:15] by Christ's death on behalf of each human person. They are now available to all who believe on the Lord Jesus Christ.

No one needs to beg or implore God for redemptive blessings. They are already provided, already paid for, already offered freely as gifts from God to all who will only believe.

All redemptive blessings may be appropriated on the same basis: They are paid for by the vicarious sacrifice of Christ; they are God's will for all who believe; they are available now; they are part of Christ's salvation.

377

God's Will Revealed

A Christian believer would never question God's will to save someone. In the same way, it is God's will to fulfill every provision that has been bought and paid for through the death, burial and resurrection of Jesus Christ. God wills:

1) To impute His *Righteousness* Section I of this book to all who believe on Jesus Christ and who embrace Him as Lord and Savior.

2) To give His *Peace* Section II to all who believe that Christ bore the judgement of their sins;

3) To provide them guidance and direction as their *Shepherd;*Section III

4) To be their *Physician* Section IV and healer of physical diseases;

5) To supply all of the needs of their lives, as their *Provider;* Section V

6) To never leave or forsake them but to always be *Present* Section VI with them;

7) To give them success and blessing for constant triumph and overcoming *Victory.*Section VII

1. God Is Your *RIGHTEOUSNESS*
Section I of this book

If condemnation or guilt besieges you with accusations about past sins, remember that *you have been washed from your sins in Christ's own blood.* ^{Rev.1:5} God sees you only in the light of *His* RIGHTEOUSNESS.

2. God Is Your *PEACE*
Section II

When despair overwhelms you and you sense accusation or intimidation or confusion or turmoil about your spiritual standing before God, remember that *Christ is your PEACE.*

3. God Is Your *GUIDE or SHEPHERD*
Section III

When problems arise and decisions must be made, when you stand at the fork in the road and need desperately to know which route to take, Christ, your *SHEPHERD*, will provide solutions and guidance.

4. God Is Your *PHYSICIAN or HEALER*
Section IV

If sickness assails your physical body and you are threatened by disease that may be incurable, count on the *Life* of Jesus your *PHYSICIAN*, at work in you, to restore your health.

5. God Is Your *PROVIDER or SOURCE*
Section V

If economic circumstances defy you and you wonder how to make ends meet, think about your Creator, your Father, who is the *SOURCE* and *PROVIDER* of all riches. He lives at your house. His wealth is yours now.

6. God Is Ever *PRESENT*
Section VI

When you feel lonely or afraid, hear Christ say, *Lo, I am with you* because He is *PRESENT.*

7. God Is Your *VICTORY*
Section VII

When the enemy bombards you with lying accusations and threats of defeat, don't forget that *the Lord is your VICTORY*. Satan must now deal with Jesus Christ when he attacks or tempts you.

JESUS IS YOURS. You are His. You and He are friends and partners. Together, you are an unbeatable team — invincible.

You have become a winner. God's legacy of blessings guarantees His best for you.

VICTORY IS RETRIEVED.

CHAPTER EIGHTY-THREE

THE PRAYER-CONFESSION

NOW, MAKE THIS confession before the Lord, claiming His victory. Say it aloud:

DEAR LORD: Before I understood why you died on the Cross, I faced problems, fears, perplexities and distress. When there was hope of winning, something always happened to rob me of fulfillment. Solutions evaded me. Success was always out of reach.

I realize that my enemy was the same adversary that robbed Adam and Eve of their paradise in the Garden of Eden.

Now *I know the Truth, and the Truth has made me free.*Joh.8:32 I know that you went to the Cross on my behalf. You met Satan face to face and endured the punishment that I deserved. You paid my account in full.

IN YOUR DEATH for me, you stripped Satan of his authority over my life.[Rev.1:18] Then you rose from the dead and lifted me out of his domain.[Col.1:13] I was *translated into your kingdom* and have been made a member of your Royal Family.[Eph.2:19; 3:14-15; 1Pe.2:9]

Now, Lord, I have heard this *Good News* and I believe it [Rom.1:16] I have opened the door of my heart for you to *come and abide with me.*[Rev.3:20; Joh.14:23; 15:4,7] You are the *Captain of my Salvation* [Heb.2:10]. I have your new *life* in me now.[Joh.3:36; 1Jo.5:12]

YOUR WORD SAYS, *If anyone is in Christ Jesus, he or she is a new creature: old things are passed away; behold, all things are become new.*[2Co.5:17]

My old sins and fears, my confusion and defeats, my diseases and sicknesses, my weaknesses and inabilities, my poverty and financial lack, my distress and failures are things of the past. They died when you died for me because *you nailed them to your Cross.*[Col.2:14]

Now instead of sins and guilt and fear, I have salvation, righteousness and peace.[Eph.1:7-13; Phi.3:9; Rom.5:1]

Instead of confusion and defeat, I have direction and success.[Pro.3:5-6; Jos.1:8]

Instead of disease and sickness, I have health and strength.[Psa.27:1; 2Co.4:11]

Instead of weakness and inability, *I can do all things through Christ.*Phi.4:13

Instead of poverty and lack, *I am rich with Christ.*2Co.8:9 God, the Creator of all wealth is my Father who wills for me His success and material blessings.

Instead of loneliness and fear, you, Lord, are now *making your abode with me* and blessing my life.

Instead of struggles and lost battles, now I am a winner because you are the *Captain of my Salvation* and I cannot lose.

MY LIFE HAS new meaning and purpose. *If God be for me* [and *with* me and *in* me] *who can be against me?*Rom.8:31 *The Lord is the strength of my life; of whom shall I be afraid* Psa.27:1

*Nay, in all these things, I am more than a conqueror through you, Lord, who loved me. For I am persuaded that neither death, nor life, nor angels, nor principalities, nor powers, nor things present, nor things to come, nor height, nor depth, nor any other creature, shall be able to separate me from the love of God.*Rom.8:37-39

PRAISE THE LORD, no enemy or power can separate me from this glorious salvation. I now live in your presence.

You said, *as many as receive you, to them you give power to become the children of God, even to them that believe on your name.*Joh.1:12 You have given me power to become your child. Now I have your *abundant Life!*

Thank you for your righteousness, peace, forgiveness, and salvation.

You are my Shepherd and my Guide, my Physician and my Provider.

You are my Source of blessings for all of my needs and you are ever present in my life, as my Deliverer and my Victory.

What a wonderful salvation! What an abundance! *What joy unspeakable, and full of glory!* 1Pe.1:8 My *VICTORY IS RETRIEVED.*

Thank you, Lord, for your message of truth that now works in me. Amen.

Chapter Eighty-Four

Pass The Good Word To Others

NOW THAT YOU have received New Life from God and have learned about His redemptive blessings, remember that all of these discoveries are seeds that have been planted in your life. They will grow and produce their harvest.

Every time you read aloud the *Prayer-Confessions* in this book, you will be watering the good seeds and they will procreate of their kind in your life.

You will begin to see circumstances around you change. It will be the harvest of God's seeds that are in your life and that you will now sow in other's lives.

Adapting To The New *Life*-Style New Thinking—New Language

This book has facilitated your understanding of what redemptive truths mean. As you reread these chapters and restate the Prayer Confessions, these truths will become solid images in your mind and spirit. Your thinking and your tongue will conform to God's way of thinking and speaking. The language of redemption will become automatic for you. In fact, you will forget how you used to think and speak. As this happens, you will find yourself acting on the basis of redemptive truths.

You will be surprised at how quickly a new world will surround you—because it begins to grow inside of you.

New *Life* Blessings

✓Friction and dissension will give way to love, harmony and fellowship.

✓Sickness and pain will fade as you learn to believe in the power of God's life in you more than in the power of disease.

✓Confusion and indecisiveness will dissipate-like a fog as you find yourself with the ability to think a situation through, to sense God's direction and to embark on a straight and good course.

386

✓The plague of poverty and unpaid bills will become a thing of the past because you will come to see yourself as a child of Royalty. You will begin to function according to God's laws of sowing and reaping. As you reach out to bless and help others, God will reach out to bless and help you.

✓Loneliness will vanish. You will discover new purpose as a member of God's Family. You will remember that Jesus never leaves you.

✓Failure and defeat will be swallowed up by new successes, because the Creator becomes your Life Partner.

AS THESE BLESSINGS spring up around you, you will realize how powerful these good seeds are. You will want to plant them in other's lives.

We Can't Keep Quiet

The richest reward on earth is to plant good seeds in others and to reap a rich harvest from your words and actions. It makes life worth living. This is what we spend our lives doing. The abundant Life of Jesus Christ is so wonderful that we cannot keep quiet about it.

Paul said, *So everywhere we go we talk about Christ to all who will listen...this is our work, and we can do it only because Christ's mighty energy is at work within us.* Col.1:28-29 LB

Sowing And Reaping

So we give our time, our efforts, our money and our energy in a constant drive to sow the good seeds of the Good News in every life we can possibly influence. As we sow these good seeds in people, our world becomes better.

Every effort we make, every gift of money we invest and every message we record or publish is another seed planted in people.

Whatever we sow, that shall we also reap. Gal.6:7

Only the seeds that a farmer plants can be multiplied back to him or her in a harvest.

Only the money that one plants in God's work can be returned to him or her in a harvest of material blessings.

Share these good seeds by planting them in other's lives so that they too can learn about God's abundant Life blessings!

Get copies of this book and plant them in other's lives. *Pass the good word on to others in need.*

THE OSBORN WORLD MINISTRY

The Osborn World Ministry

THE MINISTRY OF T.L. and Daisy Osborn has made an unprecedented impact on the world. Married at ages 17 and 18, they were missionaries in India at 20 and 21. In 1949 they instituted their organization, *Osborn Foundation*, which was later code-named, *OSFO International.* Their 510-page classic documentary, *The Gospel According to T.L. & Daisy,* with 489 photos, tells their story.

Their life passion has been: *To express and propagate the Gospel of Christ to all people throughout the world.* Their motto: One Way - *Jesus*; One Job - *Evangelism.*

For over a half century they proclaimed the Gospel together to millions, face to face, in seventy-four different nations. (Daisy died in May, 1995.) Their crusade audiences numbered from twenty-five thousand to over three hundred thousand per meeting.

Together they instituted numerous plans to reach the *un*-reached with the Gospel. They sponsored over thirty thousand quali-fied national preachers, both women and men, as full-time missionaries to their own and neighboring tribes and villages that had not yet received a Gospel witness.

Their Gospel literature is published in a hundred and thirty-two languages and their docu-miracle films, audio and video cassettes, and Bible courses for study and for public evangelism are already produced in sixty-seven languages. They have provided airlifts and huge shipments of soulwinning tools for Gospel missions and Christian workers worldwide. They have furnished scores of mobile vehicles equipped with films, projectors, giant rubber screens, generators, public-address systems, audio cassettes and cassette players, and hundreds of tons of literature for evangelism abroad.

T.L. and Daisy Osborn have both been prolific writers. Their books have helped stimulate a worldwide rediscovery of apostolic miracle-evangelism. Dr. Daisy's five major books are unprecedented in Christian literature. Her positive writing style is focused to help Christian believers, women and men alike, to rediscover their identity, dignity, destiny and equality in God's plan. T.L.'s living classic, *Healing the Sick,* already in its enlarged 42nd edition, has been a faith-building best-seller since 1951. Over a million copies are in print.

The Osborns' team efforts in world evangelism have been unequaled as they have proclaimed to the world the Gospel message that *Jesus Christ is the same yesterday, to day and for ever.* He.13:8 □